AT THE SIGN OF THE RAINBOW

MARGARET CALKIN JAMES 1895 – 1985

Betty Miles

Published by Felix Scribo

With thanks to:

Her Majesty The Queen

Nicholas and Helen Bradshaw

Jeremy and Christine Bradshaw
Benjamin Bradshaw

Ian B Calkin

Robert Riviere Calkin

Robin Calkin

Val J Calkin

Calkin, Pattinson & Co Ltd

CT Delaney

Jonathan Cape (Random House Group Ltd)

Lloyd's of London

London Transport Museum

Ann S Lord

The Worshipful Company of Scriveners

ACKNOWLEDGEMENTS

It is a remarkable satisfaction to me that this should be the second edition of this book. A great debt of gratitude is due to Betty and Philip Miles whose continued devotion to this project has been total and has both touched and inspired me. Their enthusiasm for Margaret's work has made me look at it with fresh eyes and Betty's meticulous research has uncovered facets of my parents' lives of which I had no conception. I am also very grateful to Alan Powers for his help and encouragement, and particularly for writing the Foreword. I wish my mother had known him; they have so much in common from toy theatres to pattern papers!

My thanks to the London Transport Museum in offering access to the Museum's archive transparencies and giving permission to reproduce their copyright material. In particular I would like to thank Oliver Green (Head Curator of the museum) who, in encouraging me to submit some of my mother's work for inclusion in an exhibition at the University of Brighton in 1994 on Women Designing between the Wars, sowed the seed of this entire project.

Without the encouraging response of my first sponsor, Lloyd's of London, the whole idea of a book and touring exhibition would have fallen by the wayside, so formidable was the list of refusals that followed. However, gradually friends and family became interested and have given help and they are included in the list of names opposite. A number of the family have also kindly lent pictures and other artefacts on a long-term basis. I wish especially to thank two of my cousins, Ann Lord and Robert Calkin, for their belief in me and their constant encouragement "in the cloudy and dark day" as well as for their generosity.

We would like to put on record the fact that if Hedley Picton, then head of the Art Department at the London Central YMCA, had not accepted an exhibition of Margaret Calkin James's work in 1982 and had not then written a charming article, 'Rainbow Lady' it is doubtful that Betty, Philip and I would ever have met. These so-called coincidences seem to me to have one underlying cause which continues to unfold.

Finally, an inestimable thank you to my mother, Margaret Calkin James who, through her character, example and life's work is giving enduring pleasure to so many people. This has been a most rewarding undertaking as well as being the greatest privilege I could have wished for and I hope that we have maintained the standards set by my remarkable mother whose total dedication to the work in hand never intruded on the love, joy, care and patience afforded to her family.

Perhaps the final accolade is that she has been rewarded with a comprehensive entry in the new Dictionary of National Biography.

Elizabeth Argent
December 2005

Baby Elizabeth in the arms of her mother Margaret

Title page: Margaret Calkin working at her calligraphy table, 1915

4

Margaret Calkin James, 1935.

FOREWORD

More than twenty years ago, in the springtime of the Art Deco revival, one could buy examples of the real thing, surviving in the form of Curwen Press Pattern Papers, from the Curwen Gallery in Colville Place. These were designs by luminaries like Paul Nash and Edward Bawden, commissioned in the 1920s by Oliver Simon to provide a machine-made alternative to the then-fashionable hand-blocked papers from Italy. Among the papers, one of the most attractive and jazzy was a three-colour chevron which I pasted onto the boards of a notebook. In 1987, when I organised an exhibition at Judd Street Gallery to launch the Whittington Press book on Curwen Papers, I found the name of Margaret James as the author of this design, one of the first and most successful in the Curwen range. It was only in 1994, on seeing the *Women Designing: Redefining Design in Britain between the Wars* exhibition and reading Betty Miles's catalogue essay on Margaret Calkin James that it all fell into place, for although I knew something of CH James, the architect of Wells House flats in Hampstead and many fine public buildings, history had until then overlooked his wife, perhaps the more talented of the two. The contrast reveals how in architecture the Arts and Crafts movement became conservative and classical in the 1920s, while the decorative arts, particularly the work of women, somehow retained boldness with delicacy.

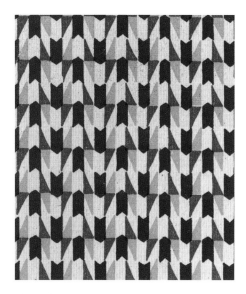

Calkin James designed this chevron pattern paper (shown actual size) for the Curwen Press in 1922.

Margaret Calkin James's designs were the most lively in *Women Designing*. She belonged to her period, as her bobbed-hair photograph suggests, but her work is still fresh, like that of her contemporaries, Susie Cooper and Enid Marx. The influence of the pre-1914 London avant-garde persists in her strong colours and delight in geometry. She also carried on the ideals of the Omega Workshops in her own Rainbow Workshops by making design into an adventure in which small things mattered as much as large and creativity was synonymous with enjoyment. Her firm principles as a Christian Scientist kept her going through her later life, when she was disabled by a stroke, yet went on designing embroideries.

It is a great benefit of feminism in art and design history that work by such artists, although not great in quantity, should be rediscovered and appraised. It has a quality that stands on its own, as Margaret James's pattern papers do in company with designs by some of her greatest contemporaries.

Needlepoint sampler designed and worked in 1980 by Calkin James (after her stroke in 1969.)

Alan Powers

MARGARET CALKIN JAMES 1895 – 1985

Margaret's mother Agnes

Margaret Calkin James was a calligrapher, graphic designer, textile printer, watercolour painter and printmaker. Her Order Book shows that she worked for the most progressive, prestigious and popular clients of the inter-war years. Her own words summarise her lifelong dedication to a functionalist ideal: 'If we would all begin at home and be satisfied with bare necessities, banishing from our lives all those things that not only are not made or fitted for a specific purpose, but that we could do without, we should then find that the country would only produce the things that mattered, that work would be done well, and the workers would be happy.'[1] This earnestness was balanced by a lively sense of humour, and with Calkin's respect for tradition came bold experimentation.

Family and Early Years

Harry Bernard Calkin married Margaret Agnes Palfrey in 1890, and Margaret Bernard, born in 1895, was the third of seven siblings, all of whom shared their father's middle name. Harry Calkin was in insurance and became a Lloyd's Underwriter in 1910; the family lived comfortably in Heath Drive, Hampstead. Reputed to be 'the straightest man in the city',[2] Harry imparted to his children his own ideals of strict personal integrity and of service to others. In this he was ably assisted by his wife, who made sure that her daughters were well versed in home economics and in patient application to hard work. Margaret's early introduction to the practical skills of cookery and needlework was an invaluable supplement to her creativity. She and her sisters attended North London Collegiate School, known to this day as a smart school for bright girls.

Young ladies like Miss Calkin were not expected to pursue a career; art, like music, was a desirable social accomplishment. Less conventional was her decision to make it her profession. Artists and craftsmen had featured in previous generations of her family. Penry Powell Palfrey (1830-1902), her maternal grandfather, carved in stone and designed church decoration, stained glass and heraldry. A skilled draughtsman, he then became a noted painter of horses for the aristocracy: his coaching scenes and Derby winners were admired by Queen Victoria, Edward VII and the Duke of Westminster.[3] On Margaret's father's side the bookbinding firm, Robert Riviere and Sons, founded by her great-grandfather, employed her uncle, Harry's brother Arthur.

Margaret's father, Harry Bernard Calkin, 1912. Detail from a portrait by his brother, Lance Calkin.
Reproduced with permission of Calkin Pattinson & Co Ltd.

Margaret's father Harry standing behind her mother Agnes with four of their seven children: Brenda on her knee; on the floor, from left to right, are Margaret, Brian and Lois.

Photograph of Margaret Calkin in 1917.

For working in her studio Calkin James always wore a blue cotton smock, replaced when necessary from a French paper pattern.

A training in fine art would have been a more likely choice for a woman of Calkin's social standing and abilities, since 'crafts' were not highly esteemed by institutions like the Royal Academy of Arts.[4] Dear old Uncle Arthur, the bookbinder, was her friend and mentor when she chose to enrol at the Central School of Arts and Crafts, where priority was given to acquiring practical skills which offered links with industry and a multi-disciplinary approach, eroding the old hierarchical barriers between fine and 'commercial' art. This pioneering institution was founded in 1896 with WR Lethaby at the helm. Calkin learned to appreciate Lethaby's outlook: her flexible, eclectic approach embodied William Morris's Arts and Crafts ideal of the well-rounded designer seeking a thorough-going reform of all aspects of the visual arts.

Calkin's progressive, independent turn of mind again emerges in her decision, during the War, to have her hair cut. Short, bobbed hair did not become common until the Twenties, but Margaret was tired of her mother's daily comment, 'Marjorie, your hair!' In dispensing with the daily dressing, coiling and arranging, she was in fact asserting her determination to lead 'the simple life'.[5] Throughout her life she made clothes for herself and subsequently for her own children that were simple, stylish and uncluttered, in keeping with her ideals.

Christian Science

Calkin's plain clothes, cropped hair and determination to live in accordance with Arts and Crafts principles caused bewilderment but ultimately no alienation from her parents.[6] During the early Twenties came another break from tradition that nevertheless forged closer ties between the generations when she, her mother, her sister Lois and brothers Ken and Alan embraced the precepts of Christian Science. These involve a spiritual discernment of reality which goes beyond the material evidence as recognised by traditional orthodoxy – a reality which Christian Scientists consider to be a present demonstrable fact in human life. 'Matter is seen not as a God-created substance but as a limited mode of human perception.'[7]

The painter Winifred Nicholson also became interested in Christian Science at about the same time: in her painting and writing about light and colour she explored these 'limits of human perception'[8]. Nicholson's work was included in 'Modern British Art' at the Whitechapel Gallery in 1923. However, although Calkin always continued to make paintings in conjunction with her commissioned design work and was sustained throughout her life in an

increasingly mechanistic cultural climate by her faith in a spiritual order, her watercolour flower studies betrayed no hint of mysticism, surrealism or abstraction and her still-life paintings and topographical landscapes were steadfastly traditional. Her modernity emerged in other forms.

Watercolour of a winter coaching scene by Calkin's grandfather, Penry Powell Palfrey, 1880. (This painting can just be seen in the family photograph on p.7)

Education and early contacts

In 1884, WR Lethaby had been one of the instigators of the Art-Workers' Guild, the first organisation of professional designers, including Ernest Jackson, Edward Johnston and Francis Troup, all of whom also taught at the Central School of Arts and Crafts. The Royal Academy shows would not admit craftwork,[9] so in 1888 they set up an alternative, the Arts and Crafts Exhibition Society. Calkin, as a student at the Central School, was therefore involved with a network of contacts devoted to design reform.

The privations of war did not prevent the Society from staging its Eleventh Annual Exhibition in 1916 at the Royal Academy of Arts in Piccadilly. Calkin was one of the students who not only exhibited work but also laboured by the side

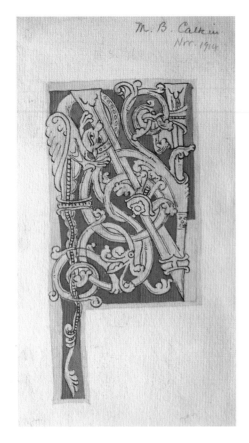

Calkin learned her craft by copying illuminated manuscripts, This small study is dated November 1914.

Detail of an illuminated manuscript copied by Calkin from the original in the V&A Museum in 1915.

of the exhibition architect Francis Troup to transform the RA galleries.[10] In a contemporary press review of the show – 'Rolls of Honour, Litanies, Canticles and so forth, penned in black or wrought in gleaming gold by that master scriptist Mr Graily Hewitt, who has an apt pupil in Miss Margaret Calkin.'[11] – she was publicly associated with an acknowledged master of the revival of calligraphy.

Indeed, the grand old men of the Guild were susceptible to Calkin's youthful zeal – half a century later she recalled in a letter that Frank Troup, at the time well into his 50s, had grown so fond as to declare his intentions. 'He wrote to mother first who had to say no (I was 19!) … he certainly was a dear!' Another admirer, whose class she attended, presented her with one of his own lithographs inscribed 'To Miss M. Calkin; souvenir of a visit to Rouen during the Great War. Ernest Jackson.'

Calligraphy

Calkin's tutor at the Central School, Graily Hewitt, insisted that a secure technique was the prerequisite for confident self-expression. All her subsequent activities were to benefit from an initial grounding in revived classical proportions and sound craftsmanship at the Central School. To these she added her own lively freedom of expression and awareness of new ideas.

The standards laid down in Edward Johnston's seminal book *Writing and Illuminating and Lettering*[12] were intended to be a flexible framework for developing the revived art of calligraphy for a new age. Anna Simons, reviewing the situation in *Lettering of Today*, 1937,[13] wrote that his fundamental principles and ideas of construction did not constrain, they liberated those who applied them afresh to contemporary design briefs: 'I know of no craft which imparts so easily and so perfectly a strong feeling for rhythm, this conspicuous feature of all modern art'.[14] Her book reproduced an example of Calkin James's book-jacket lettering as a model for modern designers (see p.59).

One sample of Calkin's work in progress was a title page for the Gospel of St John, an intricate blend of calligraphy, drawing, colouring and gilding. She submitted other completed pieces, including a Roll of Honour, to The Queen's Scholarship Competition in 1915, which she won. Karl Parsons, who had been teaching stained glass at the Central School since 1904, wrote to offer warmest congratulations, to assure her that everyone had great faith in her ability and to suggest that she 'should not continue to be so modest' about herself.[15]

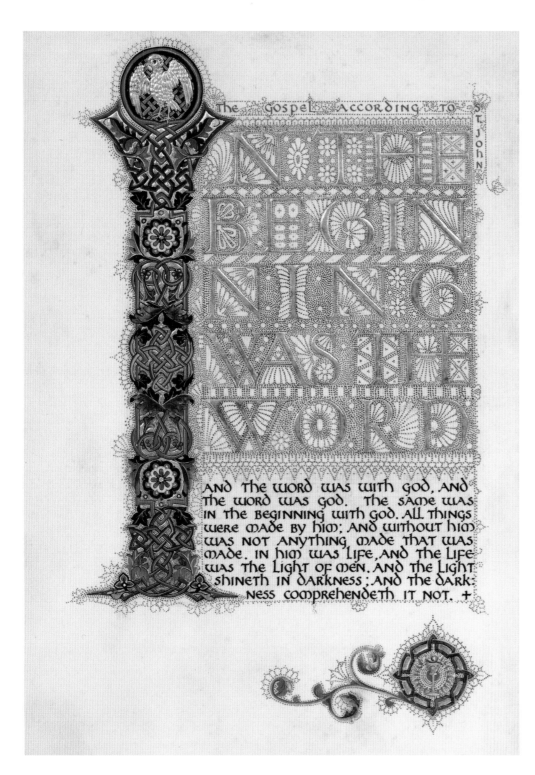

Title page of an unfinished manuscript of the Gospel of St John by Calkin James, possibly a piece of work done at Central School of Art.

Doubtless this 'modesty' was part of her charm, and of making her way as a woman in a sphere where women were vastly outnumbered. It certainly did not prevent her from tackling every opportunity that came along, adapting style, technique and scale of operation to the job in hand. There was a steady demand for calligraphy in presentation addresses, Rolls of Honour, and manuscript books for collectors. Throughout her career, Calkin also continued to design, write, illustrate and bind small volumes of verse or devotional writings for presentation to family and friends.

After Harry Calkin's death in 1926, his employers, Lloyd's of London, commissioned his daughter to write and decorate a series of loyal addresses and commemorative volumes. The first two of these volumes were bound by Robert Riviere, where Uncle Arthur worked. (It was fortunate that all these were made in duplicate: the original 1928 volume was destroyed when Buckingham Palace was bombed in 1940.)

The first volume was an 'Address from the Brokers to the Underwriters, 1928.' Its colourful illuminated and gilded titled pages, worked on vellum, depict the Lutine of 1688[16] and also great liners like the Queen Mary, then

Illuminated and gilded title page for Lloyd's 'Address from the Brokers to the Underwriters', 1928 showing the Lutine.

Illuminated and gilded text pages from the Chairman of Lloyd's 'Address to King George V., 1928.

THE ceremony to-day recalls the opening of the present Royal Exchange, when the illustrious Queen Victoria, accompanied by His Royal Highness the Prince Consort, performed the opening ceremony at the head of a distinguished company in Lloyd's Room.

IT is not without feelings of regret— that Lloyd's relinquishes its old home in that historic building after a tenancy of more than a century and a half, interrupted only by the period of rebuilding after the fire of 1838; but the whole area of Your Majesty's Capital City abounds with historic associations, & East India House, on the site of which we now stand, possesses memories not less inspiring than those which belong to the Royal Exchange. THE origin and growth of Lloyd's, constitute a strange and romantic story.

by which the name of a humble coffee-man of the 17th Century has been adopted by lines of steamers in many seas and has become a household word in many lands. It has been a long evolutionary process, during which vital changes have been made, gradually and often without deliberate intent. From the custom of a few men meeting fortuitously at a Coffee House there has evolved the Corporation of Lloyd's with its world-wide influence, needing for its home the great building which Your Majesty graciously opens to-day.

BEHIND the material development thus manifested lie those qualities of energy and character which have built up the reputation of Lloyd's, and upon the maintenance of which all else depends. Your Majesty's gracious act in coming amongst us to-day and the presence of

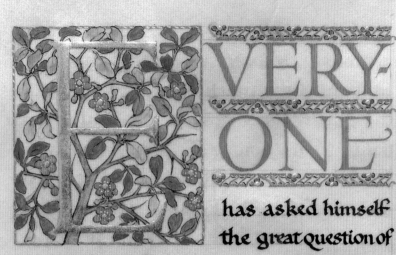

EVERY-ONE has asked himself the great question of antiquity as of the modern world : What is the summum bonum–the supreme good? You have life before you. Once only you can live it. What is the noblest object of desire, the supreme gift to covet?

We have been accustomed to be told that the greatest thing in the religious world is Faith. That great word has been the key–note for centuries of the popular religion; and we have easily learned to look upon it

4

Title page from 'The Greatest Thing in the World' by Henry Drummond, lettered and illuminated by Calkin James for her daughter Elizabeth's 21st birthday.

Illuminated and gilded title page for Lloyd's 'Address from the Brokers to the Underwriters', 1928. The stylized Arts and Crafts medievalism of the decorations and the 17th-century 'Lutine' contrast boldly with those great symbols of modernity, the ocean liners of the Cunard and Orient lines.

in their heyday. The stylized 'waves' recall the water on the Rainbow Workshops sign; the two bands of 'flames' use a device that Uncle Arthur, the bookbinder, had noticed before on a stage backdrop representing the fire in Calkin's production of Belloc's *Cautionary Tales*. These, he wrote, were a favourite ornament of the old bookbinding masters, but they had been incorporated by his niece in thoroughly contemporary 'Egyptienesque' style for the stage,[17] and

Stylized flames from the stage set of Belloc's *Cautionary Tales*, 1920 (see p.21).

Stylized waves from the Rainbow Workshops sign, 1920 (see p.25).

IT PLEASE YOUR MAJESTY,

The great building, the foundation stone
of which was laid by Your Majesty nearly
three years ago, is now completed, and it is
with the deepest gratitude that the Members
of Lloyd's on the first occasion of meeting
in their new home are privileged to have—
the high honour of Your Majesty's presence
and that of Her Majesty the Queen.

Illuminated and gilded title page for the Chairman of Lloyd's 'Address to King George V., 1928.

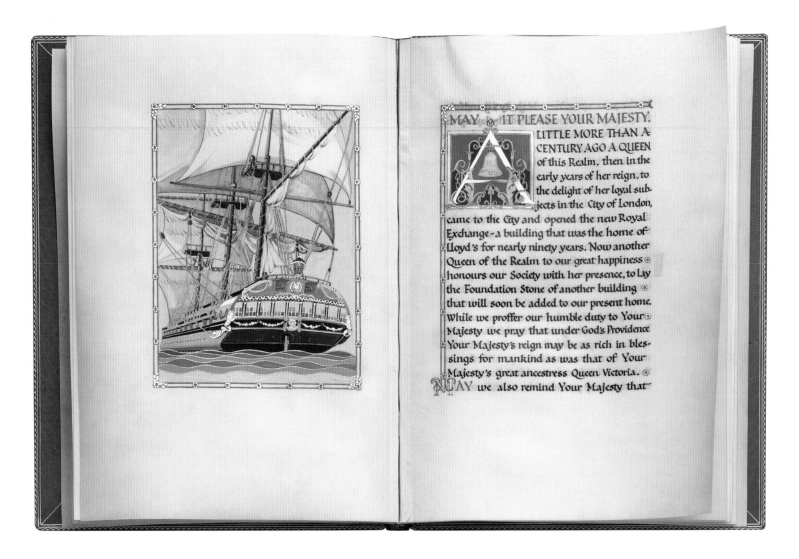

Illuminated and gilded title pages for Lloyd's 'Address to Her Majesty the Queen', 1952. The letter A incorporates the Lutine bell.

again in a blend of modern and traditional devices for the Lloyd's illuminations.

The visual and manual skills that Calkin developed initially in calligraphy were subsequently applied across a very wide range of media, with calligraphy always remaining in her repertoire. In 1921 she became a founder member of the Society of Scribes and Illuminators.

The First World War and the YMCA

War formed a melancholy backdrop to Calkin's training, and the death of her brother, Brian, killed in France in 1918, brought a personal dimension to the long lists of fallen servicemen. *The Adoration of the Soldiers*, a Christmas allegory

FOREWORD

"The Adoration of the Soldiers" is a short mystery play which was suggested to Mons: Cammaerts during a visit which he paid to the Belgian Trenches in Christmas Week. It is written in the manner of the old mediaeval French and English Nativity Plays, and with the same genuine and almost childish simplicity. In introducing the Virgin and Child among modern soldiers in a miserable dug-out, the author has endeavoured to show that the spirit for which we are fighting today is fundamentally the same as that which prompted the Crusades and erected the Cathedrals in the Middle Ages.

The English translation is by Madame Tita Brand-Cammaerts and the script has been written by Margaret B. Calkin

Foreword to *The Adoration of the Soldiers,* *(L'Adoration des Soldats)* published by Longmans, Green and Co and The Fine Art Society Ltd, 1916.

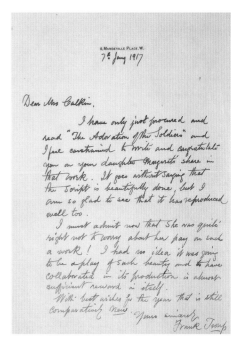

Letter from Francis (Frank) Troup.

was specially written in tribute to soldiers in the Belgian trenches by Emile Cammaerts, with illustrations by Louis Raemaekers. The lengthy text, in French and English, was penned by Calkin at no charge, including the music of an old Christmas carol and fine decorations and embellishments. The ever-attentive Francis Troup wrote to her mother in praise of the script, adding that her daughter's mere involvement in such an honourable endeavour was 'sufficient reward in itself'.[18] It was not genteel to discuss money, of course!

Troup's sentiments were in sympathy with Mrs Calkin's own outlook. Her voluntary war work for the Red Cross was considerable, even running to the invention of 'the Bracknell Night Shirt' specially designed with ties at the back for hospital patients and named after the Calkin house! She received the congratulations of Queen Mary's lady-in-waiting for being the first woman to complete 1,000 garments. Margaret's sister Lois became a nurse during the war.

Margaret herself became a war-worker *par excellence* at the Central London YMCA at 24 Great Russell Street, her first full-time job, albeit as an unpaid volunteer. Already the Central School had furnished her with skills that were previously only open to men. Even there it was commonly believed that many jobs could not possibly be done by mere women. 'Necessity, during wartime, proved to women themselves that they could do many "men's jobs" '.[19] They could even do them equally well. As head of the Art Department of the Central London YMCA she was responsible for the selection of pictures and for the design and execution of numerous decorative schemes, friezes and curtains for YMCA Red Triangle army huts overseas. Equipped with books, musical instruments, games, writing paper and envelopes as well as refreshments, these huts were a refuge for trench-bound British troops. No less than 60,000 pictures[20] and other items supplied by the Art Department, under Calkin's direction, were sent abroad to help bolster discipline, morale and team-spirit. Her prodigious efforts were hailed as 'a labour of love' and as 'a most individual contribution to the war work of the association'.[21]

Sketch by Calkin inscribed *'Cambridge House'* *Camberwell. Suggestion for stage. Y.M.C.A. Art* *Dept. Colour 2.*

Calkin and her Art Department at the YMCA continued to produce designs after the War. Early in 1920 an article in the AA Journal commended the 'many charming designs for curtains and hangings, not to speak of stencils and lithographs for wall decoration' adding that 'the YMCA Art Department scarcely meets with the recognition it deserves'.[22] Above all, it praised Calkin's stage designs for her production, in *tableaux vivants* form, of four of Hilaire Belloc's 'Cautionary Tales'.

Stage Designs and Performance

Calkin's practical training continued at an innovatory design class which had been inaugurated by Edward McKnight Kauffer at Westminster School of Art in Vincent Square. Between the Wars, McKnight Kauffer's radical innovations and genius for self-publicity did much to boost the reputation of the design profession. A few years later the effectiveness of his tuition in poster design

TABLEAUX VIVANTS
FOUR CAUTIONARY TALES AND A MORAL

HENRY KING, who chewed little bits of string and was early cut off in dreadful agonies.

REBECCA, who slammed doors and perished miserably.

JIM, who ran away from his nurse and was eaten by a lion.

MATILDA, who told lies and was burned to death.

CHARLES AUGUSTUS FORTESCUE, who always did what was right and so accumulated an immense fortune.

Produced by the Y.M.C.A. Art Department by kind permission of Hilaire Belloc.

WEDNESDAY, JANUARY 7, at 8.15 p.m.
THURSDAY,   JANUARY 8, at 8.15 p.m.
FRIDAY,   JANUARY 9, at 8.15 p.m.
SATURDAY,   JANUARY 10, at 3 p.m.

Doors Open at 7.45

Doors Open 2.30

AT KING GEORGE'S HALL
LONDON CENTRAL Y.M.C.A., TOTTENHAM COURT RD, W.C. 1

℄ *TICKETS :* RESERVED & NUMBERED, 5s. (including tax) can only be obtained from the Y.M.C.A. ART DEPARTMENT, 24, GT. RUSSELL STREET, W.C. 1.
('*Phone:* Museum 3420.)
RESERVED, 3s. and 1s. 6d. (including tax) can be obtained from the Y.M.C.A. ART DEPARTMENT, 24, GT. RUSSELL STREET, W.C. 1. ('*Phone:* Museum 3420). Also from : King George's Hall, Y.M.C.A., Tottenham Court Rd, W.C. 1; The Student Movement House, 32, Russell Square ; Y.M.C.A., 13, Russell Square ; Red Triangle Hospitality League, 25, Montague Street ; and from the following Bureaux of the Red Triangle Hospitality League : Leicester Square ; Christchurch Yard, Victoria Street, Westminster ; Melbourne Place, E. Strand.

One of four versions of the poster for the *tableaux vivants* produced for the YMCA in 1920. This version shows the lion with its 'cornstalk legs'. All the illustrations were done by Calkin with a calligraphy pen.

was reviewed in *Commercial Art*, October 1928. A poster for London Underground, 'QED', (see p. 52) by Margaret Calkin James, was accorded a full-page reproduction to illustrate the effectiveness of 'this policy of advancement'.[23] McKnight Kauffer's blending of old stability with new devices like symbolism, repetition, geometric flatness and the incorporation of good type and lettering were very much in line with Calkin's own thinking.

The class at Westminster focused on design for advertising and retailing, including posters, the use of lighting in shop windows and three-dimensional

Press cutting from *The Daily Star*, 2 January, 1920, showing Calkin (centre) with other Westminster students rehearsing the tableau 'Birth of a Pearl'.

construction of figures and sets. Most important was the weaving of these elements into a unified design. Calkin, with her pronounced theatrical bent, had quickly transferred these new concepts to stage sets, property and costume design. In January 1920 she appeared in the title role of *The Birth of a Pearl*, a tableau mounted by Westminster students for the Chelsea Arts Ball.

Margaret was not only adept at costumes, sets and props for theatrical performances and pageants – she also loved to participate. Having devised and produced Hilaire Belloc's *Cautionary Tales* in the form of *tableaux vivants* at the YMCA, with music, mime and verse, she herself played various roles including Rebecca – 'who slammed doors and perished miserably' – and

Matilda, who told lies and was burned to death. One of several illustrations by Calkin for the publicity for *Four Cautionary Tales and a Moral* by Hilaire Belloc, done with a calligraphy pen.

Press cutting from the *Daily Graphic*, 7 January 1920, showing Calkin as Matilda (right, in a wig with a long plait) in Belloc's *Cautionary Tales*. This production was held in January 1920 at King George's Hall, London Central YMCA in aid of the YMCA National Appeal.

Cardboard figures for a toy theatre. The firemen's breath shows up in the cold air!

Matilda – 'who told lies and was burned to death'. 'Firemen in Futurist Costumes!' exclaimed a newspaper headline about these 'dreadfully funny' moral tales.[24] A successful revival of the morality play 'must take modern forms and submit to modern conditions' wrote another reviewer, citing Calkin's performance as 'a model of stagecraft' and her designs as a 'direct service to popular art in England'.[25]

In addition to scenery, curtains and costumes in the very latest jazz-age style, Calkin prepared a menagerie of animals for the show, of which the most memorable and ingenious seems to have been the portentous orange lion with cornstalk legs and emerald eyes! In press reports on the final tableau about Charles Augustus Fortescue, – 'who always did what was right and so accumulated an immense fortune' – there was great enthusiasm for his parliamentary waistcoat – 'worth the price of admission alone.' [26]

There is no visual record of the *Mayflower* pageant, which opened in Plymouth then toured London and the provinces. Calkin designed proscenium

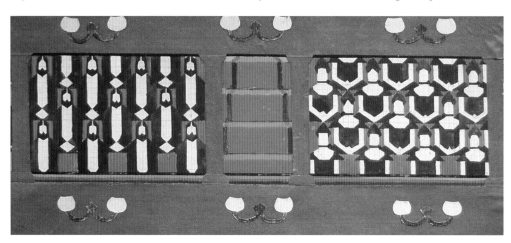

A gas-lit audience of segregated men and women, probably part of a toy theatre. Another stylized audience appears in Calkin's 'Q.E.D' poster of 1929 (see p.52).

curtains bearing the legend 'Let us now praise famous men' and 22 banners inscribed with the names of the Pilgrim Fathers with a symbol of their ship 'Mayflower' repeated throughout. In July 1920 a London exhibition of these decorations for the forthcoming pageant turned out to be the swansong of the YMCA Art Department.

The Rainbow Workshops

After the War the prejudice persisted that 'it wasn't quite normal for a woman to make money'[27] and that men needed higher wages as family breadwinners. However the experience and confidence gained at the YMCA was invaluable to Calkin and when the Art Department was closed down she took over the premises and set up her own business, retaining the existing goodwill and steadily building up a wider reputation. 'The Arts and Crafts are mustering in Great Russell Street, and each month sees a new art shop opened. The latest arrival is the Rainbow Workshop'.[28] Calkin's new venture was one of a burgeoning movement of similar businesses, like Roger Fry's Omega Workshops, that brought artists into direct contact with the public, bypassing a notoriously conservative network of wholesalers and retailers. It was also the forerunner of a number of small commercial galleries opened by women in the Twenties and Thirties to promote art, craft and design.[29]

'Beneath the rainbow on the signboard a snug little ark rides the waves, and inside the shop is as strange an assortment of beasts as Noah's Ark could boast.[30] This menagerie of animals, created for the YMCA 'Cautionary Tales', were now arranged in profusion around the Rainbow Workshops.

Calkin went on to produce sets for a one-act fantasy from the decadent Nineties, 'The Pierrot of the Minute'. The tragedy of the Moon Maiden and Pierrot takes place in the romantic Parc du Petit Trianon with a Doric temple and Cupid on a pedestal.[31] Calkin would have revelled in Granville Bantock's musical setting with piccolo, harp and glockenspiel; she herself had a fine mezzo soprano voice. CB Cochran, promoter and producer of West End entertainments, was an enthusiastic supporter of young artists and of new methods of publicity. The success of his Revue *The League of Notions*, (sending up the League of Nations that was optimistically expected to end all wars), was due in no small measure to Calkin's humorous and imaginative sets and publicity.[32]

After the War, Rolls of Honour listing the fallen provided much work for calligraphers. Such projects must have been sad for Calkin James, since she had lost her favourite brother. A roll of 2417 names of the local War dead was

Sketch for a fancy-dress costume, one example of the wide range of work produced at the Rainbow Workshops.

Ark and Rainbow symbol.
One of various permutations of this theme devised by Margaret Calkin James for letterheads and rubber stamps.

Margaret Calkin James and her husband CH James on honeymoon, 1922.

commissioned for a Brighton Roll of Honour, possibly for St Peter's Church. (Her Second World War book of remembrance is still on display at St Peter's and the pages regularly turned. Her calligraphy, gilding and illumination skills remain as fresh as ever. There is a lively sense that each name is an individual rather than one of a monotonous list, a feeling unobtrusively accomplished by the changes of colour and by simple ornaments designed to fit the varying spaces between names and ranks: another example of unity in diversity.)

With the arrival of Peace in 1918 there was also plenty of demand from private customers who wanted to redecorate their houses, attend and give parties and generally celebrate. So in Calkin's Order Book the more sober requests for Rolls of Honour and banners for charity were interspersed with orders for decorative schemes, cushions in satin, crèpe de chine, velvet and silk; lamp shades, curtains, fancy-dress costumes, stage props and 'Wig Wams'.

'Architects of taste' were advised in the AA Journal to visit the Rainbow Workshops and 'make themselves acquainted with a useful and exceptional repository of decorative craft'.[33] Artists' smocks were supplied to the Architectural Association students in Bedford Square, and as a result the architect CH James entered the Workshops in November 1920 to order a bedspread. He returned the next day to buy two lampshades. He and Margaret Calkin were married on 15th June 1922, concluding her endeavours at the premises in Great Russell Street.

House, Home and Work

CH James had married a fiesty, independent woman, who nevertheless welcomed her new role of running a home and caring for her husband. From now on she would work freelance from home as Margaret Calkin James, in purpose-designed studios incorporated into each of the houses built or converted for his family by her husband. Thus he endorsed her professional status and her studio door would be closed to family or domestic staff when she donned her smock and settled to work.

Marriage to a Fellow of the Royal Institute of British Architects who also became a Royal Academician [34] enlarged his wife's network of establishment contacts. Known to their friends as Jane and Jimmy James, the couple co-operated on some projects and had similar opinions on art and society, but in general their working lives were separate. Calkin James asserted emphatically that 'No wife can ever work with a husband at home!!'

Signboard for the Rainbow Workshops, 1920. Painted wood, double-sided, showing Calkin's chosen emblem – an ark of refuge with a rainbow of promise.

This sign, photographed hanging outside the Rainbow Workshops in Great Russell Street, appeared as an illustration in the 'Signs and Tablets' section of *Design for Modern Industry; the year book of the Design and Industries Association*, 1922.

Ark and Rainbow, flanked on each side by the rain clouds of the Deluge and Mount Ararat, where the ark came to rest after the Flood. (Genesis 8 v.4)
Margaret Calkin James installed this carved and painted wooden sign above the front door of 1 Hampstead Way.

The Design and Industries Association listed their membership and subscriptions in 'Members Rules and Activities' as follows:
JAMES, Chas. Holloway, A.R.I.B.A., *Architect*, 15 Gower Street, W.C.1. [£1.1s.]
JAMES, Mrs. M. Calkin, 1 Hampstead Way, N.W.3 [10s. 6d.].

Garden front of No. 1 Hampstead Way, designed by CH James in 1922.

CH James ran his architectural practice from four successive offices in WC2 and WC1. He had lost a leg in the War but he did not let this hinder his career and he had regained sufficient mobility to also enjoy swimming and playing cricket. His architecture had the scale and elegance of the Regency revival but incorporated all the built-in amenities and efficiencies of modern life. Honesty of construction characterised his buildings, as seen in 1, Hampstead Way, Hampstead Garden Suburb, a simple and compact three-bedroomed house he designed as their first home. Calkin James carved and painted a symbolic link between the original Rainbow Workshops and her new studio at home – a horizontal relief of the ark and the rainbow with the Deluge depicted in panels on either side.

CH James excelled in the planning of 'small houses'.[35] They were not usually so small as to exclude accommodation for domestic staff. The inclusion of servants' accommodation in the family house was as important as the provision of a studio for Calkin James, since without help it would have been impossible for her to continue with her freelance work. As a rule they had a cook and a governess (often a European refugee) and occasionally they also employed a 'house parlourman'. Even in the worst years of the Slump there was always at least one servant living in, because Mrs James's income was all the more necessary at a time when architects could find less employment.

By the end of the Twenties the Jameses had a son, Brian, and two daughters, Alison and Elizabeth. The growing family moved in 1929 to Fairway House, one of a group of homes designed by CH James in Fairway Close, Wildwood Road, NW11. Here, as always, he aspired to a feeling of considered communal development.[36] This house, with Calkin James's pleasant ground-floor studio overlooking the garden, was sold during the Depression of the 1930s and the family moved to Highgate.

In 1934 CH James was praised[37] for the admirably restrained conversion of an adjoining pair of 18th-century houses in South Grove, Highgate, one of which became their home for the next two years. The room converted to include studio space for Calkin James, was photographed (see overleaf) by Dell and Wainwright (famous for many striking images of Modernist buildings in *Architectural Review* between the Wars). The settee was a plan chest covered with a Heal's mattress, ending in a rounded cocktail cabinet. The floor was covered with large plywood squares stained silver grey and the folding doors simplified by covering them with plywood. The curtains had a large leaf pattern

Margaret Calkin James and her three children Alison, Elizabeth and Brian, seated on the terrace at Fairway House, 1929.

Living room converted to include studio
space for Calkin James at South Grove,
Highgate, 1934. The table was folded away
when entertaining guests.

Iron panel above the doorway to the garden
at 'Hornbeams'.

in the style of Marion Dorn which sat happily enough with the Persian rug; the
streamlined modernity of the fixtures and fittings also blended comfortably
with what was retained of the 18th century – the proportions of the room, the
cornice and the pattern of the glazing bars. In the narrow bathroom Calkin
James painted a beachscape mural with sand dunes and a pink and white striped
bathing tent to give a sense of space.

Finally, in 1936, CH James was able to build his showpiece, 'Hornbeams',
in Winnington Road, Hampstead Garden Suburb, N2. This 'striking example of
an architect's house'[38] was commended for the attention to detail and choice
of quality building materials. He incorporated copper drainpipes, a travertine
marble staircase, solid timber floors, doors with bronze fittings and Calkin
James's own hand-blocked fabrics, all in keeping with their ideals of sound
workmanship, honesty to materials and excellent quality. The children's
bathroom was 'pleasantly tiled in lemon, white and grey, to Mrs James's design.'[39]
Her studio, next to the large living room, opened onto the back garden. Above
the side doorway she designed an iron panel incorporating the family initials

and the date. They had only lived there for three years when war broke out. The family was on holiday in the Cotswolds, and remained there until the end of the War. CH James moved his architectural practice to 'Hornbeams' and his senior partner SF Bywaters lived there with his wife and daughter. A year later the house was requisitioned by the Royal Navy.

'Hornbeams', Winnington Road, Hampstead Garden Suburb, designed by CH James, 1936. Calkin James collaborated with her husband in the design and furnishing of this house. Photograph by CH James.

Fabric Patterns

On one previous occasion, in 1932, Calkin James's Order Book records a commission from the Edinburgh Weavers for 'Designs for woven and printed fabric repeats'. Now her fabric designs were for 'Hornbeams' and she devised a variety of abstract and floral patterns, while the more narrative schoolroom

continued p.32

In 1953 Calkin James received a request from *The Christian Science Monitor*. The Editor of the Home Forum Page wanted 'a brief story about handprinted materials'. Calkin James supplied them with three illustrations and the following text:

The printing of textiles by hand is one of the crafts that has survived the centuries.

Little has come down to us of its early history, but it is known that in the 11th-century monks in the Rhineland country were using wood blocks for printing on fabric. In England it was brought into general use at the close of the 17th century.

While the wood block method is still employed, it has been largely superseded in recent years by the introduction of the silk screen. The designer becomes conscious of the limitations that must be accepted particularly when designing for block printing, but these limitations so often contribute to the charm and distinction of the final result.

Although hand printing does not attempt to compete commercially with mechanical production, it will always have a place where the demand is for shorter lengths of exclusive designs.

The three examples are block printed fabrics designed for use in an architect's home.

The first one printed in two colours, red and grey on a natural linen ground, were executed for a children's study.

The dianthus design on wool-back satin, which is more architectural and verging on the traditional, was used with Regency furniture.

The flowered motif, printed on white poplin, was designed for a bedroom (see opposite).

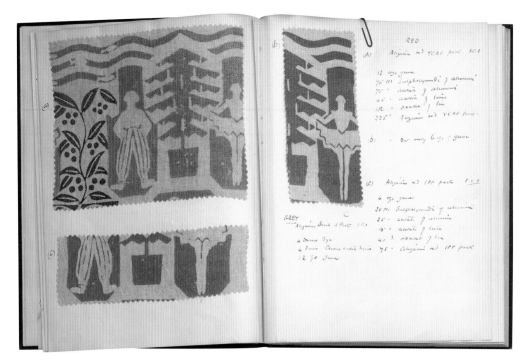

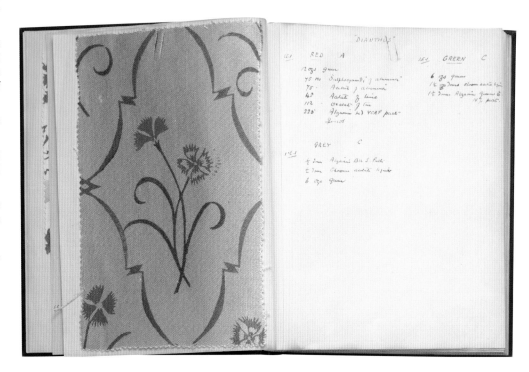

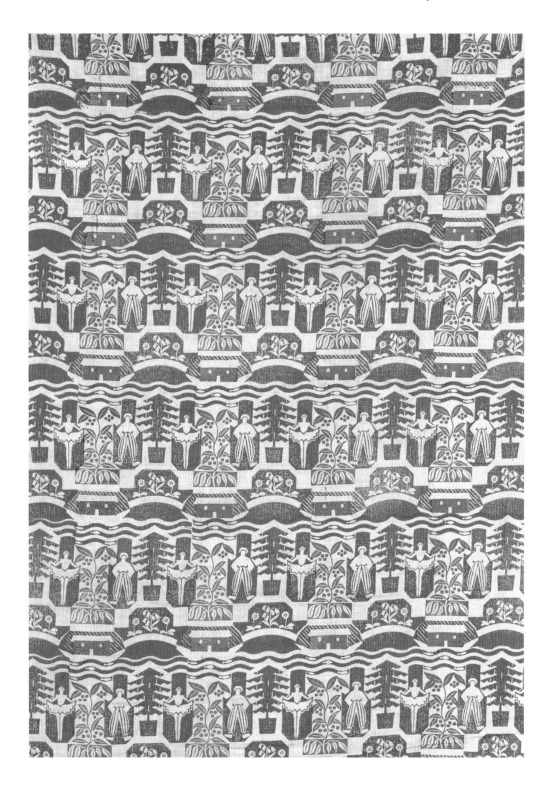

To illustrate her brief notes on textile printing by hand, Calkin James chose first this School Room fabric, which incorporates some of her favourite motifs: the ark on the waves, her stylized plant forms, a Dutch boy and a dancer, since the design was for a boy as well as girls, and a Christmas tree that reminded them all the year round of family togetherness.

Arts and Crafts gives way to Regency in her second example (opposite below), complementing the Regency furniture which CH James chose for its scale and elegance to suit the more formal rooms in 'Hornbeams'.

This large repeating pattern was designed for the master bedroom suite at 'Hornbeams'.

fabric features a signature motif: an ark floating on the waves. A large padded table was constructed in the attic at 'Hornbeams' before the completion of the house and Calkin James single-handedly printed many yards of cottons, linens and velvets to be made into curtains. (A ping-pong table fitted over this work table when the attic was used for playing games.)

The cutting of wooden blocks, the mixing of dyes (and mordants when needed), the dyeing process, followed by steaming and lengthy washings, rinsings and ironing all amounted to an arduous performance. She used a galvanised dustbin for steaming and a rudimentary gas ring for heating the dye. Quite apart from the physical labour, much research into recipes and methods was required. As Susan Bosence points out, the techniques and ideals of other countries and of previous centuries are nowadays well-documented, 'but those pioneers in the Twenties and Thirties had to find things out for themselves.'

Calkin James's methodical 'house-keeping' can be observed in her sample book of woodblock designs for fabric printing. Pattern samples in various colour options were pasted next to dye recipes; though they were designed and printed in her home for private family use, she brought her customary professionalism to bear.

Calkin James kept a book of her printed fabric samples and dye recipes from 1936 until the early Fifties.

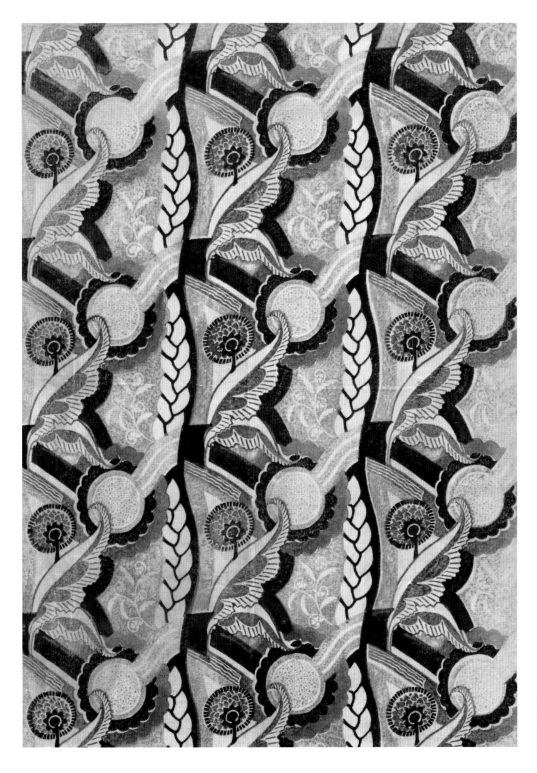

Rope and Dandelion design hand block-printed on cotton velvet by Calkin James and made into curtains for the staircase window at 'Hornbeams', 1936.

Norwich City Hall, designed by CH James and
S Rowland Pierce, 1936.
Photograph reproduced with permission from
the *Architects Journal.*

Calkin James's Rope and Dandelion design
was reprinted in greys for Norwich City Hall.

One of CH James's most important public commissions was Norwich City
Hall, designed in partnership with S Rowland Pierce (1932-38). A team of
craftsmen was employed for its construction, fixtures and fittings. Calkin's
wood-block fabric design, 'Rope and Dandelion', originally designed for the
staircase curtains at 'Hornbeams', was reprinted in a grey colourway for use in
the Marriage Suite and another of her designs was specially commissioned in
'green, mauve and red-brown' for the Lady Members' Room.[40]

Government Initiatives and Institutional Frameworks

Throughout her career, Calkin James developed a network of contacts and
benefited from various government efforts on behalf of design.

In 1921 the British Institute of Industrial Art, sponsored by the Boards of
Education and Trade, mounted the British Industries Fair, in which one of Calkin's
Mayflower banners (see p.22) was noted as an example of 'the increasing share
that women are taking', both as buyers for great firms and in the actual 'design
of things that we buy to add to the pleasure of our domestic surroundings.'[41]

Reviewing the British Art in Industry Exhibition at the Royal Academy in 1935
Herbert Read, the Modernist champion, criticised what he saw as 'costly and
depraved standards' but grudgingly allowed that the display of printing and book

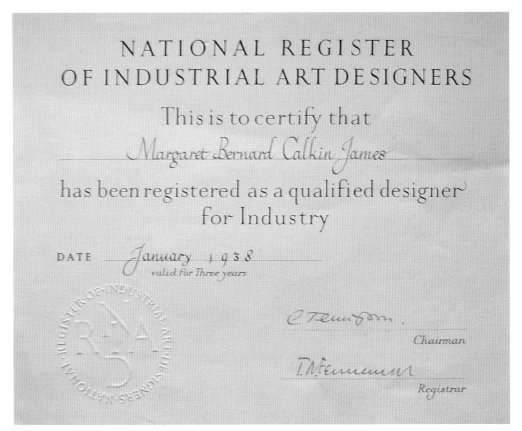

National Register of Industrial Art Designers certificate 1938.

Certificate of Commendation, RSA, 1926.

production, which included some of Calkin James's work, was 'representative of the fairly high standard which prevails in this industry' (see p. 57–59).[42]

In 1934 the President of the Board of Trade had appointed the Council for Art and Industry. The Council issued publications and arranged exhibitions to ensure that consumers, designers and manufacturers would be aware of the importance of design. In 1937 they suggested a National Register of Industrial Art Designers, which was duly implemented by the Board of Trade. Anthony Bertram trumpeted this in his BBC radio broadcasts, putting a high premium on originality and creative ability: 'Adapters and copyists need not apply'.[43] Calkin James was registered at an early stage. In January 1938 a certificate was issued to Margaret Bernard Calkin James, 'registered as a qualified designer for Industry… valid for Three years'.

In 1949 Calkin James's long-standing professional status was publicly recognized when the London County Council invited her to represent them on the Board of Directors of the Central School of Arts and Crafts. Impatient with public committees and administration, she would have declined in any case, but she was a sufficiently political animal to blench at a letter signed by the secretary of the Conservative Party. She had no wish to contribute to what she regarded as establishment complacency, though she worked within the established system for change and improvement.

Order Book

Calkin James kept an Order Book which she had begun in the Rainbow Workshops and maintained throughout her working life. A gap in this book after 1921 signalled her adjustment to family life. It also denoted the forging of her new identity as designer for the modern industrial era.

The Order Book, reopened in 1927, provides a job-by-job record of the professional life of a freelance designer working in the burgeoning post-War commercial and industrial climate. Each entry outlined the client, the brief and a deadline for completion or for submitting the rough. Occasionally dimensions were noted or an 'approx. estimate', often quoted in guineas. As each job was delivered a line was drawn through the entry.

The interchanging roles of agencies, clients and suppliers meant that the same names would reappear in the Order Book under various headings. For example, to a job recorded as 'Kynoch Press' a note was added 'Curwens to do printing'. In another entry with 'Curwen Press' as client, the job was a window bill for the Chelsea Flower Show (see p.48), ultimately financed by London Transport.

Client names were entered in the Order Book, some regularly and over many years: – BBC, Curwen Press, Empire Marketing Board, GPO, John Lane The Bodley Head, Jonathan Cape, Kynoch Press, London Transport, Lloyd's, RIBA, Shell Mex-BP, Underground. Other names appear only once: – The Edinburgh Weavers, Gas, Light and Coke Co, Institute of Mechanical Engineers, Ministry of Agriculture and Fisheries, Philips Radio, and Southern Railway. Even as a list they give a clue to the type of work she was involved in. Calkin James kept samples of only some of these completed jobs. Her entries only provide a hint of what she designed, with brief details like:– Exhibition of Architects' Drawings, 1 poster, 5 labels; Illuminated Address for London Metal Exchange; Alphabet Poster; 3 labels (produce of Scotland); Rough for Envelope for Royal Air Mail; Layout for 'You can be sure of Shell' for Petrol pumps. In addition to such corporate clients there are regular entries for commissions from private individuals. Calkin James often had to work

continued p.42

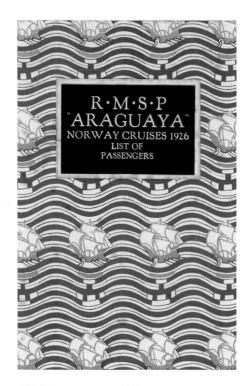

Calkin James mounted this cover onto a board with five other book covers for display in an exhibition. All six have a paper label for the title pasted onto different patterned papers, most of which are known to be from the Curwen range.

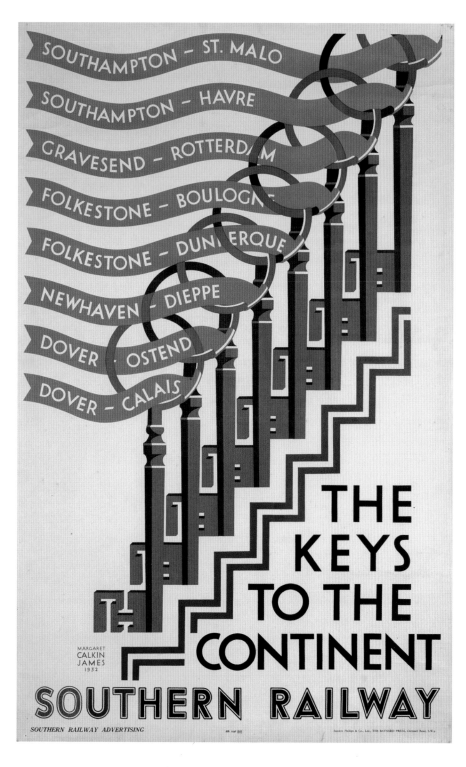

Calkin James kept a printed sample of the poster she designed for Southern Railway in 1932. The job was listed in her Order Book as 'May 30th   Southern Railway
Keys to the Continent   25 x 40'.

An important calligraphic commission, for the Coronation in 1953, was the Loyal Address from the British subjects of the Christian Science Movement presented to Her Majesty The Queen. 517 Christian Science churches and societies were listed in groups under the relevant coats of arms or badges, as researched and depicted by Calkin James.

Preparatory drawing on tracing paper showing colours used in the final illustration.

Opposite:
Calkin James's Order Book open at a sample spread from 1932.

BRITISH GUIANA

Christian Science Society, Georgetown.

HONG KONG

First Church of Christ, Scientist, Hong Kong.

JAMAICA

First Church of Christ, Scientist, Kingston.   Second Church of Christ, Scientist, Kingston.

18

April 26th. Underground Railway
Small panels for Trooping for
the Colour

May 12th. Jonathan Cape
LL series   The Magic of Herbs 34
Wordsworth 35
Typical House Spoons 36

May 30th. Southern Railway
Keys to the ...   25 × 40

June 20th. Alphabet for cloth covers
Jonathan Cape.

June 20th. Lettering sign for The Gateway
Tea Rooms. Brecon   Miss Foote.
3 Roughs + finished full size detail
of one.

June 27th. Shell Mex & B.P. Ltd.
Redesign 3 Show cards
a Scottish Paraffin Oil
b Rocklight Lamp Oil
c White Ray

June 28 Shell Mex & B.P. Ltd.
Design sign incorporating
B.P. ... Plus Roughs
+ full size drawings diameter
2' 6".

June 20th Empire Marketing Board.
... for Empire Tea Blending
(End of July)   Competition

19

Aug. 1st Jonathan Cape.
LL series 6 Jackets 37 - 42

Sept. 12th Shell Mex & B. P. Ltd.
Design for window display
Royal Standard Paraffin Oil.

Oct. 6 The Edinburgh Weavers
Designs for Woven + printed
fabrics repeats: 25 H 48 wide
36 " 48 "
by end of month (5 selection) 21g + 5g

Nov. 1st Underground.
New Station chart 11' × 2"

Nov. 19th Jonathan Cape.
2 Alphabets 6 & 7.

Nov. 26 Players Address to
Viscount Lord of Chelwood ✓

Dec. 3rd Jonathan Cape
LL series Nos 43 - 50

Dec. 3rd School of Medicine Psychology
Torrington Place
✓ 'Foundation' card for entrance hall

Tradition

This cover uses heraldry, symmetry and
a serif typeface for a Royal occasion.
It is difficult for a post-1945 generation
to envisage the hierarchical society
between the Wars, when Jubilees and
Coronations were international occasions
of genuine celebration.

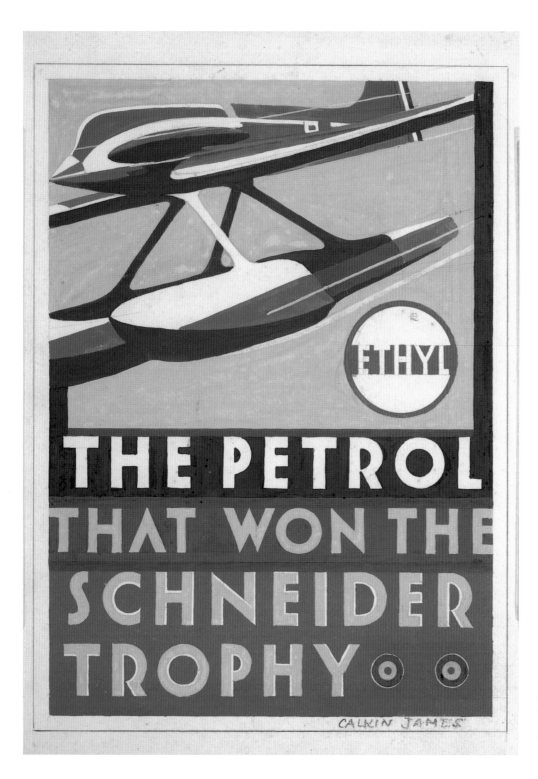

This colour rough is one of the very few surviving examples of original artwork by Calkin James.

During holidays at West Wittering in the late Twenties the James family used to watch the annual Schneider Trophy taking place off the Isle of Wight.

Modernity

Calkin James used similar colours but an asymmetrical layout and sans-serif type to create a modern image for Shell Mex. In this campaign the company laid claim to the speed, power and glamour of the new technology.

extremely hard to meet tight or overlapping deadlines.

Advertising agencies employed teams of in-house designers, but though some jobs were recorded in the Order Book under agency names:– Stuarts, APM Ltd, APEM and Regent Advertising Services – Calkin James had no regular commitment and usually worked directly for clients. Despite close contact with those who commissioned their work, designers were, as far as the public was concerned, a largely anonymous service: in 1922 the Curwen Press launched their printed pattern papers with an edition of 475 sheets of Calkin James's 'Harlequin' design, uncredited. It proved popular with publishers and bookbinders and was soon reprinted. By 1938, more than 24,000 sheets had

Two pattern papers by Calkin James from *A Specimen Book of Pattern Papers designed for and in use at The Curwen Press*, Introduction by Paul Nash, Fleuron Ltd, 1928. 'Harlequin' is the design on the right-hand page.

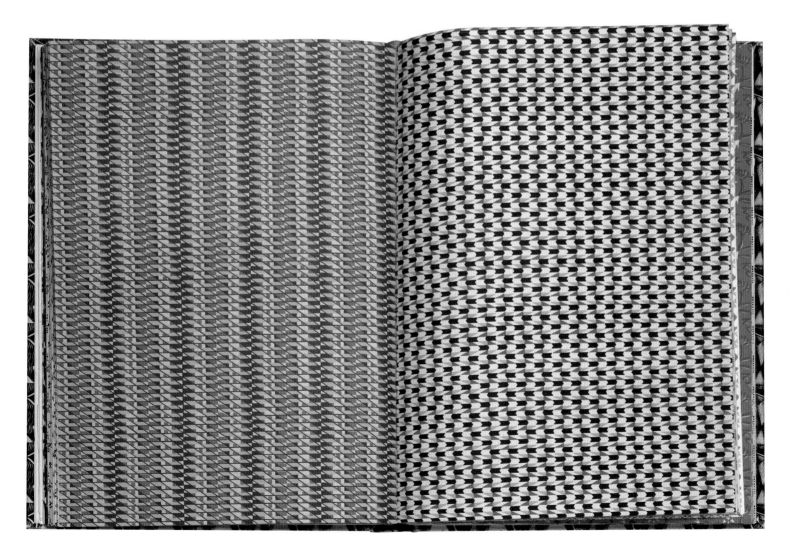

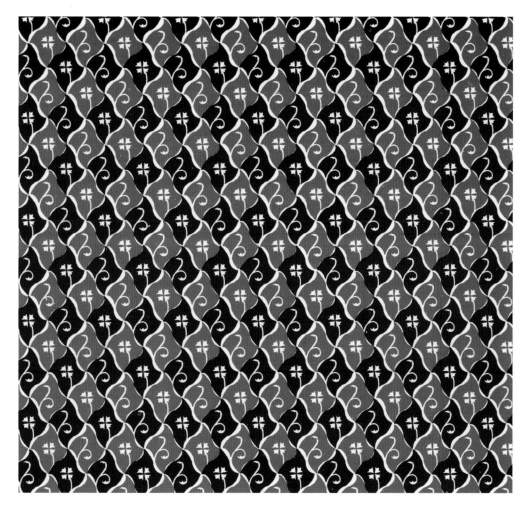

been printed. She designed another pattern in 1927 for a fee of £3-15s-7d.[44] There was no further remuneration though it, too, was in print for over half a century. Realistically, if copyright laws concerning royalties or repeat fees had been in force, the Curwen Press would not have been willing to risk imaginative ventures like these papers. Even as it was, 'by the end of 1937… receipts from sales still lagged behind the sums so far invested.' [45]

Posters and Other Graphic Design
The advantages of the poster – its size, clarity and simplicity – were never so well exploited as in the inter-War period. Poster designs by avant-garde artists, or reflecting fine art trends, were part of a new marketing drive led by

Two more Curwen Press pattern papers by Calkin James.

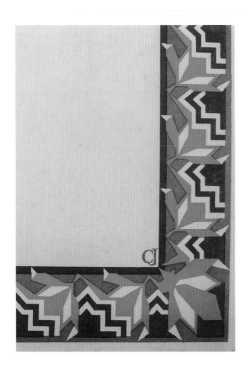

Corner detail of a double royal (40″ x 25″) border designed for London Underground in 1928, also reproduced in the Thirties in red and brown.

'a handful of high-minded autocrats' [46] – Frank Pick (London Passenger Transport Board, Empire Marketing Board), Sir Stephen Tallents (GPO, Empire Marketing Board) and Jack Beddington (Shell Mex). [47] All these clients appeared in Calkin James's Order Book as did the name of her cousin, G Grey Wornum, the architect of the new RIBA headquarters (1934). He employed Calkin James in his office for a short spell in 1928 and RIBA commissions for signs, posters, labels, cards etc. appear regularly in her Order Book, culminating in 'Prayers for Slough' in May 1937, when Slough Civic Centre, another of CH James's elegant municipal buildings, was dedicated.

The boldest pioneer of new styles in advertising was Frank Pick, as publicity manager of London Underground. Convinced of the link between aesthetic quality and commercial effectiveness, Pick established a high standard of design throughout the network in stations, rolling stock and facilities. Within these sweeping policies he allowed individual poster artists a free hand in design.

The first job for 'Underground' in Calkin James's Order Book was a Certificate for Employers in 1927. The same heading then recurred regularly above each new job from this client, as follows:– 3 borders, one double royal, 2 streamers; 2 double-crown posters 'Season tickets save time' and 'Season tickets save money'; Sketch for 'Return Journey at Single Fare; Redraw Theatre Poster; Prepare rough for small poster… Armistice Day; Panel for Christmas; Christmas Card; Panel poster 'Bluebells'; Panel poster for Royal Tournament; Small poster for Trooping of the Colour; New station chart.

In 1933 the various transport networks were integrated as London Passenger Transport Board, with Frank Pick in charge. Calkin James's job listings were now under 'London Transport' or 'LPTB': – D.C. poster 'Let it be said when you have been, You keep the face of nature clean'; Redesign certificate for Lambeth North Training School; Poster D.C. 'Kenwood'; D.C. poster 'Boxhill'; 4 D.C. posters … 'Hampton Court', 'Kenwood from Parliament Hill', 'Greenwich', 'Wood Green Swimming Pool' and finally, in January 1935, this time under the heading 'Curwen Press':– Design for Chelsea Flower Show. Window bill L.P.T.B.

The Underground was crowded during rush hours but Pick wanted people to use the off-peak service, so many posters did not focus on the transport itself, but on the marvellous places and events that could be reached by train in leisure time. Kew Gardens, Boxhill and Kenwood were places thus promoted; Trooping the Colour and the Royal Tournament were two such

Panel poster 1931
© London Regional Transport.
Courtesy London Transport Museum.

events. Calkin James's contrasting posters for these two grand occasions illustrate her adaptation of style to content (see overleaf). Both had the flatness and immediacy that called attention to their message. 'Trooping the Colour' (1932) had well-drilled rows of vertical soldiers in red on a sober pavement, yet the blue band and the central Union flag lent an air of pageantry. For 'Royal Tournament', the other event promoted by Calkin James that year, a single image of uniform size was repeated, overlapping, in two rows. There was no illusion of depth, only an animated pattern of colour and movement across the surface, denoting the promise of action and excitement, and banners crossed to lead the eye forward. The letters, freely adapted from classic forms, are also tipped forward in agreement with the theme, while those in 'Trooping the

Royal Tournament 1932
© London Regional Transport.
Courtesy London Transport Museum.

Trooping the Colour 1932
© London Regional Transport.
Courtesy London Transport Museum.

Chelsea Flower Show, 1935.
© London Regional Transport.
Courtesy London Transport Museum.

Colour' stand up straight and tall like soldiers on parade.

Pick's willingness to give artists a free hand earned the tube platform the title of the poor man's picture gallery.[48] Through advertising, the conservative British public became visually adjusted to the formal devices that had first appeared in the paintings of Cézanne, the Cubists and the Futurists. It did not happen all at once since the public found even a poster like 'Kenwood' (see p.50) exceedingly 'modern'. As a pair, 'Kenwood' and 'Box Hill,' appealed to the English vein of nostalgia for the leafy rural scene; the sunny landscapes were organised into formal arrangements of flat harmonising colours. These pictures appear conventional nowadays but to the public between the Wars they looked decidedly non-naturalistic.

Even more 'modern' was Calkin James's poster 'Bluebell Time' in which she transformed the delicate observations of her water-colour studies into flat patterns, sharp contrasts and repetitive forms for instant impact. In 'Q.E.D'

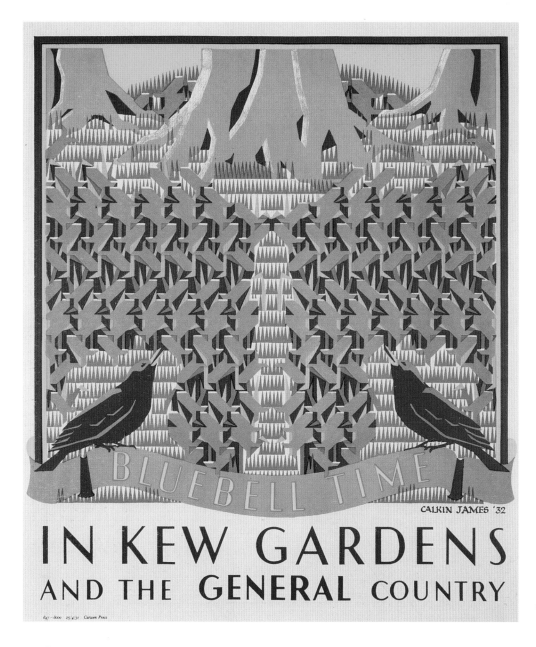

Bluebell Time, 1932.
© London Regional Transport.
Courtesy London Transport Museum.

(see p.52) Calkin James skilfully incorporated well-groomed passengers travelling by tube to join the audience for a spectacular West End chorus line-up. Authoritative bold capitals, strong horizontal bands, symmetry on a strict geometric grid and unusual colours were all combined to give an astonishingly lively effect.

Box Hill 1935
© London Regional Transport.
Courtesy London Transport Museum.

Kenwood 1935
© London Regional Transport.
Courtesy London Transport Museum.

Q.E.D 1929
© London Regional Transport.
Courtesy London Transport Museum.

Wood-block printed Christmas cards, willow
c.1948, poppy 1930s.

Calkin James designed and printed Christmas cards to send to her family
and friends as well as to clients. Frank Pick wrote, on Christmas Eve 1938,
'Your card so much excels itself as a card that it deserves a letter of thanks,
for the much time and great care you have given to it...'.

Pick was equally discerning of print quality on an industrial scale. He
ensured that his designers had the back-up of excellent printing: firms like
Waterlows, the Dangerfield Printing Company Limited, the Baynard Press and
the Curwen Press all provided a high-quality service. Designers like Calkin James
had to tailor their visual ideas to the limitations as well as the possibilities of the
lithographic process.[49] Her contact with the Curwen Press led to miscellaneous
smaller jobs such as some lively postcards for Barrows Stores in Birmingham
(1937) which represent groceries and how they can be enjoyed.

Christmas card c.1936, based on pond plants
at 'Hornbeams'.

During the Twenties Frank Pick was also on the publicity committee of the
Empire Marketing Board under Sir Stephen Tallents, who shared Pick's belief
that good design meant good business. In 1933 Tallents was transferred to
become the first Public Relations Officer of the General Post Office. The
standard black bakelite telephone had been replaced (in 1929) by a new urea
formaldehyde moulding that could be produced in a range of colours, some of
which proved unpopular or did not wear well. By 1935 the final range was

established as chinese red, ivory, jade green and black and these remained standard for the next twenty years. To launch them, Calkin James was commissioned to design a poster urging the public to 'consider your colour scheme'. She united all four colour options on one poster by the artful use of the same drapery in different colourways.

In the same year Tallents launched a new marketing idea for the GPO: the Greetings Telegram, 'to end the popular superstition that a telegram means bad news'.[50] Calkin James was asked to design the first one of these, with a matching design for the envelope. The space for the message was surrounded by a sprightly border of traditional interlaced ornament, doves carrying envelopes, stylized branches and a bottom line of musical notes in red, gold and blue, Reminiscent of manuscript illuminations, the design was variously ascribed in the newspapers of 23 July 1935 to 'an artist', 'a woman artist' and 'the artist Mrs M.C. James'[51] Tallents sent her a sample of the handbill that was to announce the new service in 'some 23,000 post offices all over the U.K. tomorrow morning', adding in an accompanying personal note that she 'deserved' to have

Greetings Telegram, 1935.
Calkin James's proposal of similar decorative elements on a white envelope to match the telegram was overruled by the GPO who insisted on an envelope with a gold printed background, which obscured her design.

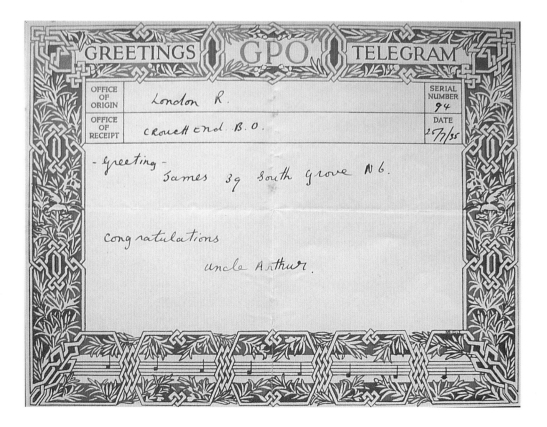

Poster for the GPO to promote the new range of coloured telephones.
Courtesy The Robert Opie Collection.

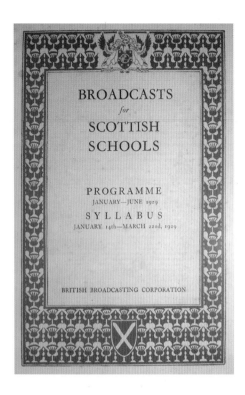

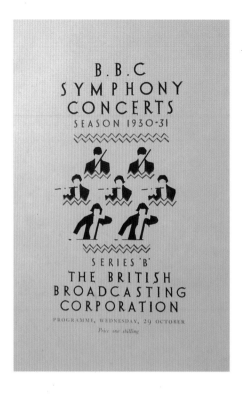

Covers for the BBC, 1929 and 1930–31

a copy.[52] Evidently the new service was popular and later designs were commissioned from a wide variety of artists including Edward Ardizzone, John Farleigh, Barnett Freedman and Robert Gibbings.

Calkin James was never content to settle for a 'good enough' design or a formula to fit all briefs. Two BBC commissions serve to show how adaptable she was in the search for an appropriate solution. A booklet, 'Broadcasts for Scottish Schools', used a sober, serif type face carefully centred and balanced by heraldic devices top and bottom: the strong border pattern of purple thistles and leaves added a light-hearted 'Scottish' flavour. Equally suited to its theme was a BBC Symphony Concerts programme: these letterforms were distinctly modern and in keeping with the bold, black shapes, each repeated to suggest an orchestra.

Book Jackets

Designs for book jackets span the whole of the inter-war period and were another field in which Calkin James excelled. Legibility was the fundamental requirement, but she lent distinctiveness by creating hand-drawn letterforms or written scripts and flourishes to suit the individual character of each title. These were accompanied by a relevant ornament, a stylized illustration or laid out in a 'box' superimposed on a pattern. To arrive at these patterns the constant discipline of objective drawing[53] as well as her innate selecting eye enabled Calkin James to pare things to their essential elements.

The knack of reduction, describing the subject and simultaneously forming an abstract pattern was daringly employed on book jackets such as *Lothian Cameron, The Bull Fighters*, and *General Crack*. The large-scale repeats left 'windows' for the book titles that were designed to hold their own against such striking backgrounds.

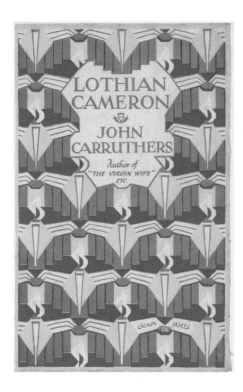

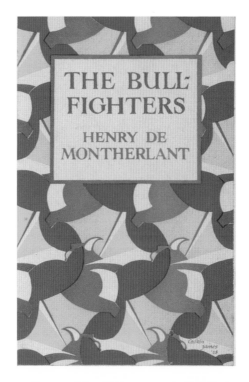

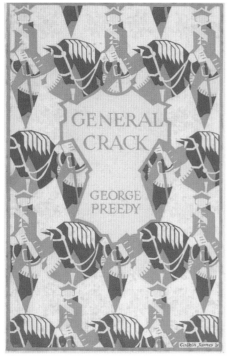

General Crack designed for John Lane
The Bodley Head, 1928

Lothian Cameron, *The Bull Fighters*, 1928
Young Mrs. Burton, 1954
Designed for Jonathan Cape.
Used by permission of the Random House Group Ltd.

Calkin James always read the book before
designing an illustrated jacket.

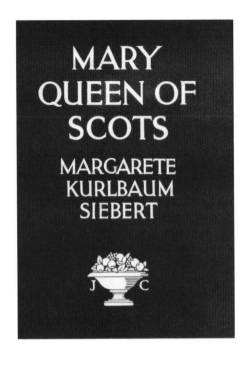

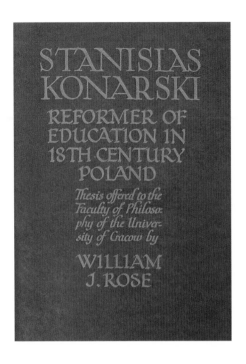

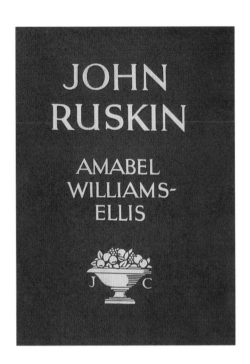

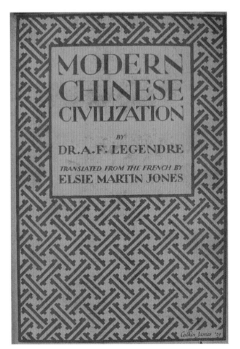

To draw the eye and hold the interest can, on the other hand, be a very subtle and quiet art, using well-spaced lettering and careful layout alone. Calkin James designed alphabets for use on cloth covers and on book-jackets for Jonathan Cape, including jackets for *Juan in America* and *Juan in China*. Altogether she designed six alphabets for Cape. Her aim, learned from Edward Johnston, was always to make good letters and to arrange them well. From 1930-37 Calkin James designed book-jackets for the *Life and Letters* series, using a typographic solution to which she brought a great deal of subtle variation. Originally intended as a series of 14, this eventually ran to more than 70 volumes.

Jonathan Cape's founding partner was G Wren Howard, who was a neighbour of the Jameses in Hampstead. Wren Howard was responsible for the appearance and production of the firm's publications. Calkin James's work over two decades measured up to his high standards of craftsmanship and design and also those of John Lane at the Bodley Head. She not only designed lettering and layouts for their books but also labels, leaflets, press advertisements and showcards. All displayed the characteristics of the English typographic reform inspired at first by William Morris and subsequently by the private presses at the beginning of the twentieth century.

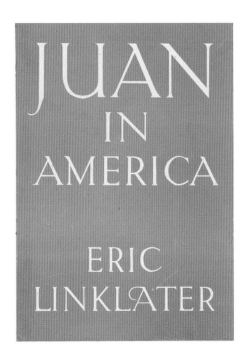

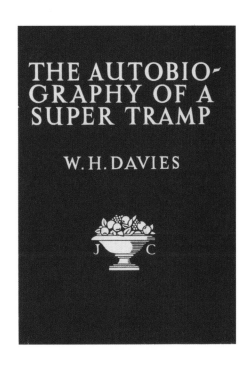

Book jackets for Jonathan Cape.
Used by permission of the Random House Group Ltd.

In 1935, Calkin James mounted two boards of her book jackets for display in the Printing and Book Production section of the British Art in Industry Exhibition at the Royal Academy of Arts (see page 35).

A double-page spread from *Lettering of Today* (1937) illustrating an article 'Lettering in Book Production' by Anna Simons.
In this selection of successful modern jacket designs, *Juan in China* by 'Mrs Calkin James' appeared along with some of her eminent male contemporaries, including Barnet Freedman, Lynton Lamb, Francis Minns and Berthold Wolpe.

Rural Retreats and the Second World War

In keeping with their ideals of rural simplicity, the Jameses had rented Barn Cottage in West Wittering, Sussex for summer holidays during the Twenties and Thirties. In 1939, the family was on holiday at Lapstone Farm in Chipping Campden when the Second World War broke out. CH James asked the farmer's wife, Mrs Badger, if they could stay another week. This agreement turned into an arrangement that lasted over two years. Their son Brian was at boarding school and the two girls were accepted at Campden Grammar School.

Calkin James's freelance design career was on hold, though she continued with her watercolour studies, which had always been woven into the pattern

Watercolour inscribed 'Panorama of Lapstone Farm, Campden, Glos. Oct.1943

of her life. She joined the Womens's Land Army in 1940 but some months later when a WLA inspector came to Lapstone Farm and found her baking bread – an activity not considered WLA work – she was fired! She continued to work in the Badger's garden and walked the three miles each way to work in Gordon Russell's garden at Kingcombe, near Dover's Hill. (CH James knew Gordon Russell and his furniture through professional contacts in London.)

For the Artists' General Benevolent Institute, she made forays to John Lewis's salvage sales in London to buy bolts of material in order to run up multiple small dresses and shorts for children orphaned in the Blitz. Her daughter recalls each little garment going off with a penny in the pocket.

View from Dover's Hill, Chipping Campden, over the Vale of Evesham. Watercolour, 1943.

Mixed bunch of garden flowers
Watercolour and gouache, 1938

Later, when Birmingham and Coventry were devastated by bombs, Calkin James organised a weekly supply of a gross (144) of terry-towelling squares for nappies. Every Campden Grammar School girl took one home to be hemmed and returned each Monday and packed back at Lapstone Farm – a job often interrupted by a descent to the cellar during air-raid warnings – then

Opposite:
Sweet peas (from the garden at 'Hornbeams')
Watercolour and gouache, 1938

sent to the Red Cross depots in the bombed cities.

In 1942 the family moved to Miles House, Chipping Campden, which they rented fully-furnished until the end of the War in 1945. This house had been restored at the beginning of the century by CR Ashbee, when he took his Guild of Handicraft away from the East End of London to live and work in the Cotswolds. In Campden, Calkin James was close friends with Professor MacKail (biographer of William Morris) and his wife Margaret. The two Margarets often sang madrigals and folksongs together, with Mrs MacKail playing the Bechstein piano at Miles House.

When his office had to close, CH James, along with many other RIBA and RA colleagues, joined the Camouflage Directorate at Leamington Spa. So many artists managed to affiliate themselves with this unit that this small Midlands town had 'the greatest concentration of artists anywhere in Britain'.[54] CH James's disability from the First World War entitled him to some petrol coupons which enabled him to return to the family in Chipping Campden at the weekends. Their eldest child, Brian, went to Clare College, Cambridge for a year-long Officer Training Course and then joined the RAF. Tragically, he was killed in action just a few months before the War ended.

Greater Celandine
Watercolour study, c.1940

Exhibition private view card, 1935

Watercolours, Exhibitions and Prints

Freshness, 'economy of means and a quite remarkable purity of colour'[55] were the hallmarks of Calkin James's watercolour landscapes, still life paintings and flower studies. At the Cooling Galleries in New Bond Street, London in 1935 her 50 flower studies, 'accurate and delicate as botanical plates, were so popular that red discs looked like confetti flung about the exhibits.'[56] Her old admirer Francis Troup, now in his 70s, wrote to reserve no.46, 'Chicory', adding 'I can then have coffee in the pot and Chickory [sic] on the wall'. Calkin James usually exhibited calligraphy and illuminated books with her watercolours; thus a note addressed to her husband from his Arts Club crony CFA Voysey expressed his 'sincere congratulations on the splendid exhibition … especially the designs and illuminations'.

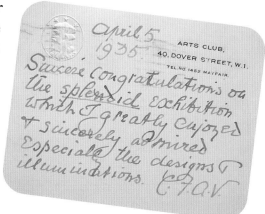

Mixed bunch of garden flowers
Watercolour, 1940
Inscribed 'To Ellen Badger'

Rhododendron 'Pink Pearl', painted at
Cannon Cottage, Hampstead, 1950s

In the Cotswolds during the War, Calkin James painted watercolour landscapes and over several years prepared a collection of wildflower studies to accompany her handwritten anthology of poems. Her selected authors, 'from Pliny to the present day',[57] were either concerned with a spiritual quest or with evocations of rural life, such as 'some wizard quotes from Vita Sackville-West's poems especially The Land. … I have also got hold of the Collected Poems of Mary Webb.'[58] A selection from this 'Flower Anthology' was shown at Kensington Art Gallery in January 1948 as part of the exhibition 'Watercolours and Flower Studies by Margaret Calkin James'. A patchwork quilt, 'designed and executed by the artist',[59] was displayed in the same case.

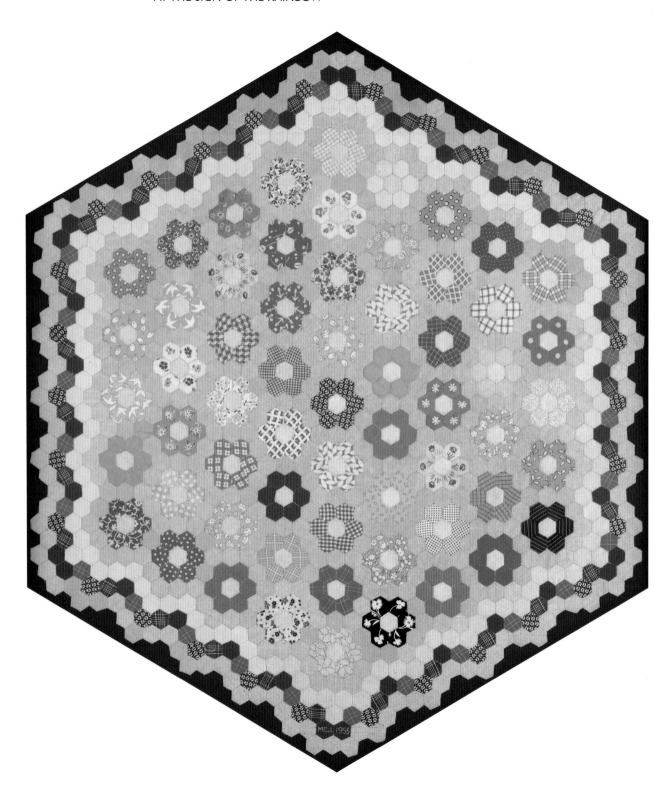

Watercolour of columbines and 'Ming' painted at Cannon Cottage, 1950. Calkin James bought the doll for 5 shillings in the Caledonian Market in 1938 and then made shoes and silk clothes for it.

A selection of 18 examples from the Flower Anthology was included in her exhibition 'Flower Studies in Water Colour' at St Georges Gallery, Cork Street, London in May 1957. A reviewer contrasted her work with Edward Burra's watercolours at the nearby Lefevre Gallery. Burra's showed the 'new and exciting things to be done by the modern flower painter',[60] whereas Calkin James's approach was 'more accessible to the average buyer ... graceful and charming, exquisitely truthful ... they cannot fail to please.'[61]

Calkin as a 'modern' flower painter had created the 'Chelsea Flower Show' poster in 1935, when she heightened colours and emphasised strong lines and dominant patterns, imposing a designer's agenda. These later flower studies had a different purpose, a straightforward personal response to the variety and

Opposite: Hexagonal patchwork sewn by hand from scraps, with MCJ 1955 embroidered in one corner. Each hexagon is only about 5/8ths of an inch across.

SOW THISTLE

And weeds that bloomed in summer's hours,
I thought they should be reckoned flowers:
They made a garden free for all,
And so I loved them great and small,
And sung of some that pleased my eye,
Nor could I pass the thistle by,
But paused and thought it could not be
A weed in nature's poesy.

John Clare

The 'Flower Anthology', a volume of original watercolours and handwritten poems, bound together in the 1970s.

richness she observed in living plants. The strength of her seemingly anonymous documentary approach is its sensitivity and truthfulness. The work did please reviewers, but to her lasting disappointment the 'Flower Anthology' was not reproduced. It was frustrating that in the austerity of the post-War period no publishers or private press was willing to risk the expense of creating 'the de luxe edition which it certainly deserves.'[62] The proposed book remains unpublished and was eventually leather-bound for her by her daughters as a unique volume of poems and flower studies.

The only commercial outlet for her flower paintings was a request from the Medici Society, which published two sheets of Calkin James's studies as

prints in 1957. The colours had to be crudely 'bumped up' to allow for the technical limitations of colour reproduction and also for prevailing market tastes. The last exhibition listed in the Order Book was in 1961 at the Medici Galleries.

Calkin James continued to print her own woodblock cards of flowers for friends and family and her linoprints were regularly exhibited and sold at the annual Royal Academy Summer Exhibition. The linoprint blocks retained in the family archive show her painstaking precision: as many as nine separate colours would

WITH ALL GOOD WISHES
From Mr. and Mrs. C.H. JAMES

Top left: Dandelions.
Proof from a woodblock print, undated.

Top: Snowdrops.
Christmas card, machine printed, c.1935.

Above: Snowdrops.
Christmas card, linoprint, 1952.

Left: Mermaid Rose.
Linoprint, c.1968.

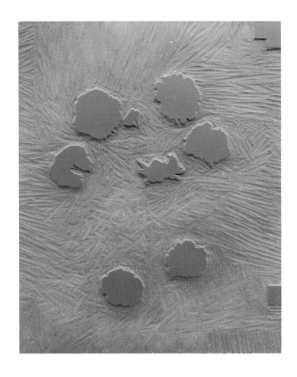
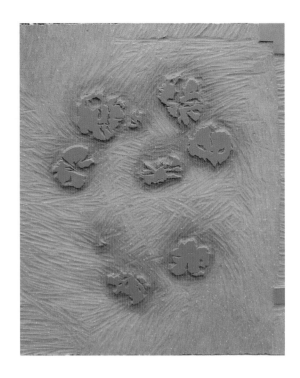
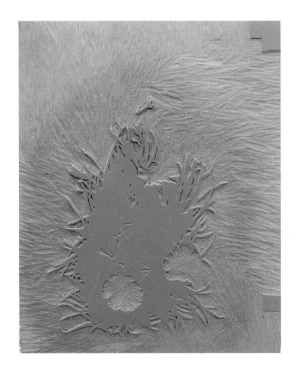
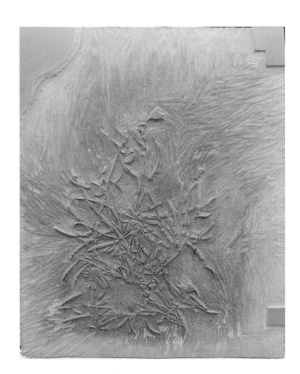

Dianthus 'Doris'
Linoprint in nine colours from separate
blocks, four of which are shown opposite.
Exhibited at the Royal Academy of Arts
Summer Exhibition, 1966.

Study from a sketchbook.
Pencil and watercolour, 1965

Cyclamen.
Linoprint. Exhibited at the
Royal Academy of Arts
Summer Exhibition, 1965.

be carefully combined to create a deceptively fresh and subtle image. These prints were again based on observed and often quite ordinary reality but the alchemy of printmaking provided yet another dynamic to her pictures.

After the Second World War

When the War ended and Hornbeams was vacated by the Royal Navy in 1945, the family returned, to remain there until CH James's death, aged 60, in 1953. The house was then sold and Calkin James and her unmarried daughter Elizabeth made their home in Cannon Cottage, Well Road, Hampstead. The garden façade of this house was blank brick, a perfect site for Calkin James's *trompe l'oeil* painting of a sash window being opened by a maid, presumably to tend to the window box, also depicted. This convincingly real 'window' caused neighbours to look twice. 'I didn't have a maid either,' she ruefully remarked, 'so that was another bit of wishful thinking'.[63]

Once again, with the Peace came some melancholy work for Calkin James, especially poignant since she had lost her own son: she undertook

Pastel portrait of CH James by James Grant, 1945.
Courtesy RIBA Library, Drawings & Archives Collection

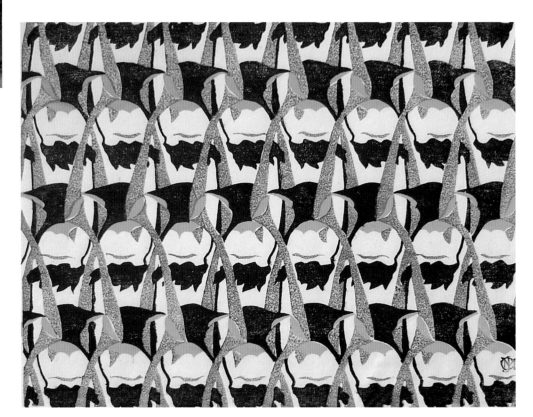

Penguins
Linoprint, c.1962.

Calkin James made this study for the *trompe l'oeil* window at Cannon Cottage using her daughter Elizabeth as a model.

The black and white photograph was taken in the 1950s, when the window was first painted. The maid – named Perpetua by the family – was dressed in 18th-century costume to match the period of the house. The colour image shows the window as restored in 2002 by the present owners.

Watercolour study of a building site,
(location unknown).
Page from a sketchbook, 1950s.

Unfinished watercolour of Tenby.
Sheet from a portfolio, c.1935.

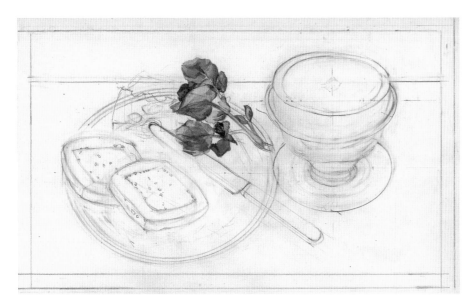

Pencil and watercolour study.
Page from a sketchbook, 1950s.

'A Light Lunch'
Tempera on prepared board, c.1955.

commissions for two Rolls of Honour, one in 1950 for Gerrards Cross Parish Church and another in 1961 – listed as '2 wars 13 names' – for Hampden in Buckinghamshire. The last entry in her Order Book was in 1962, 'Memorial leaflets 24 copies' for Lady Drysdale of Onslow Square, SW3.

The Will to Conquer

Calkin James lived and worked in Cannon Cottage for 17 years, continually painting, printmaking and exhibiting her work. A piece from this period is one of only two tempera paintings she completed (see p. 77): she taught herself the technique with advice from Eliot Hodgkin who visited her at home.[64] In her 70s Calkin James went by bus to lithography evening classes at Hornsey College of Art. By this time her daughter Elizabeth was married and living at Cannon Cottage with her husband and two young daughters.

In 1969 a stroke deprived Calkin James of speech and the use of her right hand. Even then, this indomitable maker wanted to handle shapes and colours and to create. The many small wool samplers she worked in needlepoint with her left hand were a means of continuing with her pattern-making and expressing her delight in visual experience. They 'grew in technical competence

Four wool embroideries selected from around.200 worked by Calkin James, showing her developing control as she learned to use her left hand after a stroke.

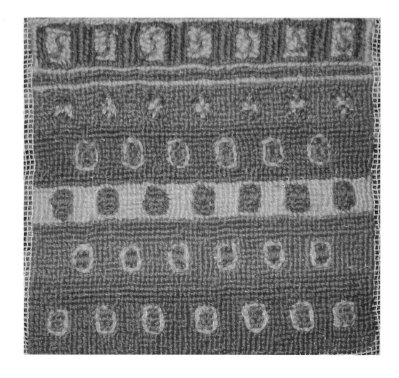
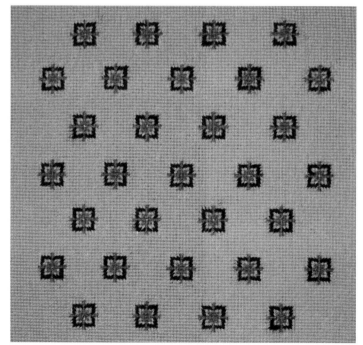

Calkin James photographed for the *Welwyn Times*, November 1981, to publicise her exhibition of wool embroideries.

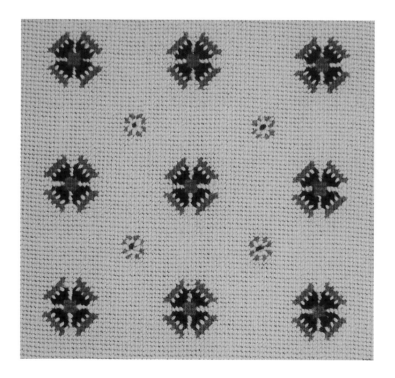

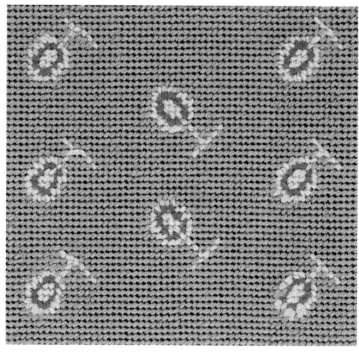

… but even the early heavy-handed examples display the strength and sensitivity of an experienced designer.'[65] She enjoyed this means of expression almost to the end of her long life.

After Calkin James was disabled, Elizabeth's family moved in 1970 from Cannon Cottage to live in a larger property in Welwyn, with ground-floor accommodation for her mother. It gave Calkin James great pleasure in 1981, the International Year of the Disabled, to see her wool embroideries displayed in the Central Library at Welwyn Garden City. The following year, a larger exhibition of her work was displayed in the exhibition 'Rainbow Lady', held at London Central YMCA in Great Russell Street 60 years after she had closed the Rainbow Workshops in the same street!

Margaret Calkin James died in 1985. Since 1996, an exhibition of her work has travelled to various venues throughout England, including Burgh House, Hampstead (restored by CH James as part of a post-War housing development). 'Thoroughly Modern Margaret', a feature in *The World of Interiors*,[66] was followed by the commercial reproduction of a selection of her 1930s fabrics.[67] In 2004 she was deemed worthy of a comprehensive entry in the *Oxford Dictionary of National Biography,* as one of the 'remarkable people in any walk of life who were connected with the British Isles'.[68]

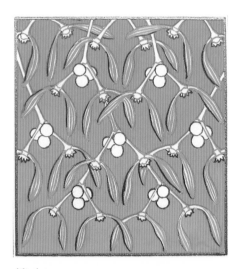

Mistletoe
Handpainted design in gouache and gold
c1950s.

Handpainted pattern, possibly from the
Rainbow Workshops, c.1920.

Calkin James and her husband both found early in life the principles they would build upon professionally. One of CH James's obituaries stated that 'he never got entangled in new ideas. He perfected and simplified the one he understood.' [69] In 1921 the 'good work' being produced by Miss Margaret B Calkin in her Rainbow Workshops was praised in *Colour* magazine for its 'keen attention to the requirements of modern life'.[70] Also reviewed – coincidentally on the same page – were the 'daring experiments' in architecture being carried out by her future husband, CH James. Both of them had the conviction that 'beauty is a consequence of purpose perfectly fulfilled'. [71]

Margaret Calkin James had a sense of purpose in her life which gave great verve and confidence to any work she undertook. Her designs had a relaxed and unlaboured quality and her colour sense was intuitively sound. The recurring themes of Ark and Rainbow signified for her a refuge and a hope, in line with her sincere commitment to the ideals and teachings of Christian Science. These accorded well with the precepts of the Arts and Crafts Movement and were the impetus behind her consistent pursuit of simplicity, usefulness and beauty.

Silkscreen-printed handkerchiefs, showing two of several colourways, c1950.

Silkscreen-printed silk scarf, showing one of several colourways. Calkin James made these scarves out of war-surplus silk parachutes, which dictated the triangular shape.

Notes

1 'Notes of the Month', *Colour*, October, 1921, Vol.15, No.3, p.vii.

2 Obituary, *The Times,* 1926 (undated press cutting filed by Calkin James).

3 'The late Penry Powell Palfrey', *Baily's Magazine*, October, 1902, p.231.

4 The Royal College of Art began as a school of design but even there the fine arts of painting and sculpture were far more prestigious. Peggy Angus, who began her training at the RCA Painting School, was conscious of 'a great loss of caste' when she transferred to the Design School. Carolyn Trant, 'An Interview with Peggy Angus', Jill Seddon and Suzette Worden (Eds.), *Women Designing: Redefining Design in Britain Between the Wars,* University of Brighton, 1994, p.99.

5 This reshaping of accepted attitudes was 'never for the simple-minded'. Fiona MacCarthy, *The Simple Life*, Lund Humphries, 1981, p.9.

6 Dora Carrington, another 'product of the protected suburbs', entered the Slade in 1910 and had her hair cut soon afterwards to assert not only artistic freedom but also personal independence from her parents and an angry rejection of bourgeois conventions. Gretchen Gerzina, *Carrington*, John Murray, London, 1989, p.19.

7 *Encyclopaedia Britannica,* 1984, quoted by Judith Collins, *Winifred Nicholson*, Tate Gallery, London 1987, p.18.

8 Ibid.

9 John Brandon-Jones, 'WR Lethaby and the Art-Workers' Guild', Sylvia Backemeyer and Theresa Gronberg (Eds.), *WR Lethaby, 1857-1931; Architecture, Design and Education*, Lund Humphries, London, 1987, p.26.

10 Peter Rose, 'It Must Be Done Now: The Arts and Crafts Exhibition at Burlington House, 1916', *Decorative Arts Society Journal*, No.17, p.4.

11 'The Arts and Crafts Exhibition: Pleasure, Profit and Patriotism', *Glasgow Herald*, 31 November, 1916.

12 Edward Johnston, *Writing and Illuminating and Lettering*, Sir Isaac Pitman & Sons, Ltd., London, 1927. The Artistic Crafts Series of Technical Handbooks, edited by W.R. Lethaby.

13 Anna Simons 'Lettering in Book Production', (Ed.) C.G. Holme, *Lettering of Today*, The Studio Ltd., London, 1937, p.57.

14 Ibid., p.58.

15 Letter from Karl Parsons, dated July 1, 1915: 'My dear Miss Calkin, Marjorie told me that she had heard from you that you have had private information of your success in the Queen's Scholarship Competition. I am aware that you did not wish me to be told until it was officially announced, but since I have known it from the very day of the judging! perhaps you will condone my impatience in offering you my best congratulations without further delay. I saw the show, and I consider that no sensible judges could have decided otherwise. It would be as useless, I know, as it would be ill-advised to tell you not to continue to be so modest about yourself, but I do hope you won't go on suggesting to yourself that there are certain things which you can't do. We hear a lot about 'The will to conquer' in these days: I'm sure this delightfully unexpected success – unexpected by you, that is, will help you to cultivate it! I would dare wager that I'm not the only one with plenty of faith in your ability. Sincerely yours, Karl Parsons.'

16 The ship's bell was recovered from the Lutine and re-hung on the rostrum of the Underwriting Room at Lloyd's. It was traditionally struck when news of an overdue ship arrived – once for bad news, and twice for good news. The bell was sounded to ensure that all brokers and underwriters are made aware of the news simultaneously. The last time it was rung to tell of a lost ship was in 1979 and the last time it was rung to herald the return of an overdue ship was in 1981. It is now rung for ceremonial purposes to commemorate disasters such as the 9/11 disaster, the Asian Tsunami, the London Bombings and is always rung at the start and end of the two minutes silence on the anniversary of Armistice Day. http://en.wikipedia.org/wiki/Lutine (accessed 20 December, 2005).

17 '... the fire scene, representing the end of Matilda, was admirably rendered by means of a black curtain with a border of formal flames rising about two feet from stage level.' 'Colour Design on the Stage', *The AA Journal*, Vol.XXXV, No.396, February, 1920, p.247.

18 Frank Troup, letter to Mrs Calkin, 7th January, 1917.

19 Caption to a 1916 photograph of women setting up type, Maureen Hill, *Women in the Twentieth Century*, Chapmans, London, 1991.

20 *Queen,* 13 November, 1920.

21 Ibid.

22 *The AA Journal*, February, 1920, ibid.

23 'New Talent: The Westminster School of Art', *Commercial Art*, Vol.V, No.28, October, 1928, p.178. Also mentioned in this review was Calkin James's friend and contemporary Frank H. Dowden who had taken over the class from McKnight Kauffer.

24 *Star*, 2 January, 1920.

25 B.B., 'Moralities', *The Challenge*, 16 January, 1920, p.173.

26 Press cutting 'Belloc Parodies in Tableaux' (unattributed, undated, filed by Calkin James).

27 'Enid Marx RDI: and Interview', Helen Salter, *Women Designing*, ibid., p.92

28 *Queen*, ibid.

29 Notably the Three Shields Gallery in Kensington owned by another Central School calligrapher, Dorothy Hutton; Muriel Rose's Little Gallery, and later, Dunbar Hay. Hazel Clark, 'Selling Design and Craft', *Women Designing*, ibid., p.58.

30 *Queen*, ibid.

31 'Notes of the Month', *Colour*, ibid.

32 'Mrs Calkin James … ne contribua pas moins à son succès par le sens humoristique de sa fantaisie et de ses multiples idées tant picturales que plastiques.' (unattributed French magazine article filed by Calkin James.)

The League of Notions, by John Murray Anderson and Augustus Barratt, with music by Augustus Barratt, was produced by Charles B. Cochran at the New Oxford Theatre, London, on 17 January, 1921.

33 *The AA Journal*, February, 1920, ibid.

34 CH James: Associate of the Royal Institute of British Architects 1918, Fellow of the Royal Institute of British Architects 1926, Associate of the Royal Academy 1937, Royal Academician 1947, Fellow of the Royal Society of Arts 1951.

35 Obituary, *The Times*, 10 February, 1953.

36 CH James considered the context for every type of building: 'a little 1930 factory off Savile Row by CH James, where the plain building face of good proportion, was sensitively attuned to the differing heights of buildings on either side'. HAN Brockman, *The British Architect in Industry 1841-1940*, p.148.

37 'Two Houses in South Grove, Highgate', *The Architects' Journal*, Vol. 80, 5 July, 1934, p.10.

38 *Journal of the Royal Institute of British Architects*, 10 January, 1938, p. 239. See also Randal Phillips, 'An Architect's Own House', *Country Life*, 5 August, 1939, p.121.

39 *Journal of the Royal Insitute of British Architects*, ibid.

40 'Norwich City Hall', *The Architectural Review*, November, 1938, p.216.

41 'Some Feminine Interests', *The Daily Telegraph*, 26 February, 1921.

42 Herbert Read, 'A General Impression of the Exhibition', *The Listener*, 9 January, 1935, p.51.

43 Anthony Bertram, *Design*, Penguin, London, 1938, p.111.

44 The unequal treatment and the commercial exploitation of famous names is underlined in Fiona Hackney's article 'Women at Curwen', *Women Designing*, ibid. p.51.

45 David McKitterick, *A New Specimen Book of Curwen Pattern Papers*, The Whittington Press, Gloucestershire, 1937.

46 David Bernstein, 'Introduction', *The Shell Poster Book*, Hamish Hamilton, London, 1992.

47 Roger Fry, writing for *The Spectator* in 1923, had seen the potential for posters to 'redress the balance in favour of art.' Most manufacturers were not bold enough to have artists designing their mass-produced textiles or pottery, but the ephemeral nature and relative cheapness of posters were an encouragement to the industrialist to take risks. Roger Fry quoted by Mark Haworth-Booth, *E.McKnight Kauffer: a designer and his public*, Gordon Fraser Gallery Limited, London and Bedford, 1979.

48 Wyndham Lewis quoted by Mark Haworth-Booth, ibid., p.22 and p.30.

49 Colour photography would later tempt designers to simulate reality too exactly, thus losing the impact of the more symbolic interpretations. Armin Hofman, 'Thoughts on the Poster', Dawn Ades, *The 20th-Century Poster*, Abbeville Press, New York, 1984.

50 *The Times*, 23 July, 1935.

51 *News Chronicle*, *Daily Mirror* and *The Times*, 23 July, 1935.

52 Stephen Tallents, letter to Mrs James, 30 July, 1935.

53 For example, in 1926 she had attended life drawing classes taught by her friend Ernest Jackson at Byam Shaw School of Art.

54 Between 150 and 200 artists were working there and the Artists International Association established an Artists and Designers' Collective, including Richard Carline, Robin Darwin, Stephen Bone and Julian Trevelyan.
Lynda Morris and Robert Radford, *The Story of the Artists International Association 1933-1953*, Museum of Modern Art, Oxford, 1983, p.65.

55 *The Times*, 24 April, 1935.

56 *Birmingham Post*, 18 April, 1935.

57 Letter from Calkin James to her daughter Elizabeth, 3 September, 1944.

58 Ibid.

59 Catalogue, 'Watercolours and Flower Studies by Margaret Calkin James', Kensington Art Gallery, 13 to 31 January, 1948. (Printed by Hague and Gill, at Pigotts, High Wycombe). The back page listed the display as follows:–
Case 1: Illuminated books
(Description under each).
Case 2: Flower anthology, Patchwork quilt, designed and executed by the artist.

60 *The Lady*, 16 May, 1957. The same review goes on to mention Eliot Hodgkin (*see 64 below*) as an exhibitor in 'Flower Paintings by Artists of Today' at the Medici Society's Milne Gallery.

61 Ibid.

62 James Burr, 'English Flora', a review of Calkin James's exhibition at St George's Gallery, *Art News and Review*, 11 May, 1957.

63 Press cutting, 'A window in paint', *Hampstead & Highgate Express* (undated, filed by Calkin James).

64 Eliot Hodgkin (1905-1987) was a painter, best known for his egg-tempera still-lifes. He studied at Byam Shaw School of Art and at the Royal Academy Schools under Ernest Jackson.

He taught mural painting at the Westminster School of Art.

65 Hedley Picton, 'Rainbow Lady', *YMCA Central News*, 17 February, 1982.

66 Rupert Thomas, 'Thoroughly Modern Margaret', *The World of Interiors*, September, 1997, p.106.

67 Five 'exquisitely simple and elegant designs of Margaret Calkin James ... taken from samples kept by her daughter Elizabeth Argent.' *Borderline presents The Calkin James Collection*, Chelsea Harbour Design Centre, London, Spring, 1998.

68 Betty Miles, 'James, Margaret Bernard (1895-1985)', HCG Matthew and Brian Harrison, (Eds.) *Oxford Dictionary of National Biography*, Oxford University Press, 2004. http://www.oxforddnb.com/view/article/75304 (accessed 1 January, 2006).

69 Arthur Kenyon, CBE, FRIBA, 'Obituary, CH James', *The Builder*, 13 February, 1953, p. 264

70 *Colour*, ibid.

71 *Colour*, ibid.

Curwen pattern paper (see p.36).

Betty Miles trained as a painter/printmaker at Birmingham College of Art, and practised for some years as an artist and illustrator. As a part-time pottery teacher at London Central YMCA she helped to display the work of Margaret Calkin James at the 'Rainbow Lady' exhibition of 1982 (see p.80) and met the artist. She recalled this 'Rainbow Lady' ten years later when she heard about a proposed exhibition of forgotten women designers. As a postgraduate student in the History of Art and Design at Brighton and Sussex Universities she contributed to the exhibition and publication *Women Designers Between the Wars* in 1993. Her article on CH and MC James was published in the *Journal of the Decorative Arts Society*, no. 20, 1996. She has lectured on Margaret Calkin James at various exhibition venues and contributed an account of her life and work to the *Oxford Dictionary of National Biography* in 2004. Meanwhile she continues with her own drawing, painting. and printmaking.

Alan Powers is Reader in Architecture and Cultural History at the University of Greenwich.

First published 1996 by Felix Scribo.
This revised and enlarged edition published 2005 by Felix Scribo
2 Arrow Grange, nr. Alcester,
Warwickshire B49 5PJ
01789 764272
email: elizabethargent@tiscali.co.uk
www.margaretcalkinjames.co.uk

A CIP catalogue record of this book is available from the British Library

ISBN 0-9528481-1-2
978-0-9528481-1-0

Printed by G&B Colour Printers, Hanworth
Designed by Philip Miles, Brighton

FELIX SCRIBO
SCRIPSI FELICIOR
Margaret Calkin James

Happy I write
Happier I have written